Why Do Bad Things Happen To So-Called "Good" People

Douglas C. Hoover

Beautiful Feet Outreach Ministries
San Diego, California
858-715-8442
email: doug@beautifulfeetoutreach.com
website: beautifulfeetoutreach.com
website: watergardenauthority.com

Why Do Bad Things Happen To So-Called "Good" People
by Douglas C. Hoover

Printed in the United States of America

ISBN 978-1-60477-765-9

www.xulonpress.com

Dedication

I dedicate this book to my beloved wife and best friend, Alice Susan Hoover. Alice was not just a major support of my work on this book, but she has been an inspiration to me by her dedication to the daily service, worship and witness for our Lord and Savior Jesus Christ. Her child-like faith and unconditional love for God is demonstrated in her attitude about life and in the way she treats other people in many different situations. I'm blessed to be called her husband and her best friend also.

Contents

Preface

If my interpretation of the Book of Job is scripturally correct, then the readers of this book will discover truths about God's nature and character that will stretch their faith and challenge many of their preconceived notions and paradigms. Prior to studying the Bible on my own, I would rely on Bible scholars, teachers, preachers and evangelists to interpret the Word of God for me, placing my trust and faith in their ability to *"rightly divide the word of truth."* When I began to question the accuracy of several things I heard, and decided to search it out for myself, I discovered serious discrepancies in their interpretations. *So then faith comes by hearing, and hearing by reading and speaking the Word of God.* **Romans 10:17** *God's Word is a lamp for my feet, and a light for my path.* **Psalms 119:105** *I study to show myself approved by God, a servant that is not ashamed, correctly interpreting, understanding and speaking the truth of the Word of God.* **2Timothy 2:15** *If I ask, it will be given to me; if I seek, I will find; and if I knock, God's knowledge, revelation and wisdom will be opened unto me.* **Luke 11:9**

Because our faith in God comes by reading His word and my main purpose in writing this book is to build up your faith, I have not only used hundreds of scriptures, I have repeated specific verses several times in several chapters. It has been said that the best preachers and speakers in the world use a technique that is effective in learning. They will tell you what they are going to tell you, then they will tell you, then they will tell you what they just told you. That way you will hear it three times, and the technique of repetition is paramount in the process of learning and memorization.

Consequently, I will repeat some scriptures and extremely important concepts several times throughout the course of the book. May God richly bless you through the reading of this book and may the truth of God's word be revealed to you and may the truth set you free.

Introduction

You may not have read the book of Job yourself, however you may have heard one or more opinions from various pastors or theologians. Some say that the book of Job was a contest between God and Satan, to determine Job's devotion; others say that God allowed Satan to test Job's patience or that He allows suffering so that your spirituality will be complemented by your learning some kind of lesson. Matthew Henry, the well-known late 17th century minister and theologian, states in his commentary on Job, "The permission God gave to Satan to afflict Job was for the trial of his sincerity." The most important question to be answered in the book of Job is whether or not God did give Satan permission to test Job.

Romans 10:17 says, *Faith comes by hearing, and hearing by the word of God.* Consequently, the more of the Word of God that you read, the better you will understand God. The more you know about God, the easier it is to believe what He says and establish your faith in Him. If you understand God to be something other than what He is, your faith will be twisted and non-effective. The purpose of this book is to give you new hope, by revealing to you the truth about the book of Job. I truly believe that what I have learned from the book of Job has changed my life in every respect. It has changed the way

I look at God, the way I worship Him, my faith in Him, my ability to receive healing and health, answers to my prayers, my desire to serve Him and place all of my trust in Him.

What I am about to share with you in this book should give you great hope and much joy. Looking back over the account of Job's life, you read what appears to be one of history's most unlikely, unqualified candidates for receiving the wrath of God. The big question is, did he receive God's wrath? Before answering that question, answer this one: What was God's opinion of Job's character? Let me help you out: **Job 1:8** And *the Lord God said unto Satan, Have you considered my servant Job, that there is none like him in the earth, a perfect and an upright man, one that fears God, and shuns evil?* Now let me get this straight: God is perfect, His judgment is perfect and righteous, and He judges Job to be perfect and upright. This same God is now supposed to enter into a wager or bet with Satan or even allow this vile, disgusting being to test Job or orchestrate a trial against him. I beg you to appeal, just for a moment, to your God-given wisdom and Godly sense, letting go of the life-long, adopted, preconceived religious and worldly-motivated paradigms and notions. Could you trust a God that says and promises one thing and then demonstrates and delivers the opposite?

I thank God for showing me that there are more than two ways to look at something. Rather than assume that someone did something one way or another, consider the option they had nothing to do with it at all! It has been said, "A man with experience is not at the mercy of a man with an argument." **John 9:25** ... *One thing I know, that whereas I was blind, now I see.*

CHAPTER 1

The Wager

After several years of contemplation and soul-searching and praying for a divine revelation on the **Book of Job**, found in the Old Testament of the Bible, I have come to the conclusion that my first suspicions were correct. I will share them in this chapter, but first I must lay a foundation.

Jesus Christ claimed to be not only the Son of God, but God himself. **1John 5:7** *For there are three that bear witness in heaven: the Father, the Word, and the Holy Spirit; and these three are one.* **John 17:21** *...that they all may be one, as You, Father, are in Me, and I in You; that they also may be one in Us, that the world may believe that You sent Me.* **Psalms 107:20** *He sent his word, and healed them..."* Jesus bore witness to the character and nature of the Father God, and His life itself was the personification of God. Jesus testified to the goodness, holiness, righteousness, justice, purity, amazing grace and tender mercies of God the Father. Jesus warned us of Satan's power and of the fact that in **John 10:10** *the thief [Satan] comes not, but for to steal, and to kill, and to destroy: I am come that they might have life, and that they might have it more abundantly.* Jesus was not quick to share the precious truth of the word of God to those men who were proud, arrogant, self-righteous and stiff-necked; for that reason, when speaking in public, He hid the truth in parables. For those who are willing to seek the truthand accept the truth, they will find it. **Matthew 7:7** *Ask, and it will be given to you; seek, and you will find; knock, and it will be opened to you.*

One principle Jesus spoke on regularly was the power of our words: our words can bless or curse, create or destroy, build up or tear down, encourage or discourage; it is totally up to us, by our free will, what we choose to speak. Jesus taught that we can create our own environment by choosing our words wisely and the words we choose can be rooted in fear or in faith. God's Word teaches us that, *out of the abundance of the heart the mouth speaks.* Therefore, it is paramount that we fill our hearts with God's Word and by doing so we are building up our faith and also speaking faith-filled words. Our thoughts control our speech and this truth is evidenced by the Bible's exhortation: *Cast down arguments and every high thing that exalts itself against the knowledge of God, bringing every thought into captivity to the obedience of Christ.* (**2Corinthians 10:5**) *Finally, brethren, whatsoever things are true, whatsoever things are honest, whatsoever things are just, whatsoever things are pure, whatsoever things are lovely, whatsoever things are of good report; if there be any virtue, and if there be any praise, think on these things.* (**Philippians 4:8**) Man, prior to God sending His Word in the flesh, which was Jesus Christ, had a disadvantage in not knowing the truth about Satan (the adversary) and about the importance of the words we speak, either giving Satan permission or God permission to inter-vene or intercede in our lives.

Answers to life's most pertinent and persistent ques-tions can be answered by the truth, knowledge and wisdom contained in the Word of God. *But we preach Christ cruci-fied, unto the Jews a stumbling block, and unto the Greeks foolishnes.; Because the foolishness of God is wiser than men; and the weakness of God is stronger than men. But the natural man receives not the things of the Spirit of God: for they are foolishness unto him: neither can he know them, because they are spiritually discerned. For the wisdom of this world is foolishness with God. For it is written, He catches the wise in their own craftiness.* **(1Corinthians 1:23; 1:25; 2:14; 3:19)** *Professing themselves to be wise, they became fools.* **(Romans 1:22)**

There are many preachers, pastors, evangelists and Bible scholars that profess themselves to be wise. In my opinion, it is an awesome responsibility for a teacher or pastor to accurately interpret the story of Job because as goes the Book of Job, so goes the entire Bible. If you misinterpret Job, your interpretation of the whole Bible, more than likely, will be affected. The disease of misinterpretation will infect your faith in divine healing, protection and prosperity. People who believe God gave Satan permission to test Job by terrorizing him, killing his family and destroying his possessions have a hard time believing God for much of anything. God's character and nature hinges on one important question: Did God give Satan permission to test Job? No matter how you pose the question or phrase it, the outcome is the same: God played a direct role in Job's incredible suffering.

I have spent untold hours searching the internet trying to find just one advocate that agrees with me. Agrees with me about what? Before I answer that, let me pose a few questions. Is it possible that… **1.** God did not give Satan permission to test Job? **2.** God did not even allow Satan to test Job? **3.** God had nothing to do with Satan's test of Job? **4.** It wasn't a test at all? and **5.** Job himself gave Satan permission by his fear-filled words? *For the thing I greatly feared has come upon me, and what I dreaded has happened to me.* **(Job 3:25)**

God asked Satan, *"What do you think of my servant Job? Have you considered my servant Job, that there is none like him in the whole earth, a perfect and an upright man, one that fears God, and shuns evil?* **(Job 1:8)** *So Satan answered the LORD and said, "Does Job fear God for nothing? Have You not made a hedge around him, around his household, and around all that he has on every side? You have blessed the work of his hands, and his possessions have increased in the land. But now, stretch out Your hand and touch all that he has, and he will surely curse You to Your face!"*

Now pay very close attention to what God did not say: He did not say, "Go ahead, test him." Or did God simply make an observation and then state the observation? *"Behold, all that he has is in your power; only do not lay a hand on him."*

Now at this juncture in the narrative, many theologians and Bible scholars take gross liberties in adding to or embellishing the Word of God. Matthew Henry states on page 7 of his commentary on Job that God said, "all that he has is in thy hand, make the trial as sharp as thou canst; do thy worst at him." This is **not** paraphrasing, but rather **gross conjecture**. Matthew Henry, much like many preachers or teachers of the Bible, approaches Scripture with an agenda. They tend to study the Scripture through the lenses of preconceived ideas and notions, taking care not to disturb or shatter their pre-existing paradigms.

Let's assume for a moment that it is God's will for our bodies to be free from sickness and disease, and that Jesus not only took our sins upon the cross, but also, our disease, sickness and infirmities: *and by his stripes we are healed.... God sent his word and healed them.... Thy will be done on earth as it is in heaven.* Even though there are dozens of scriptures to prove that God wills us to be healthy, I will refrain from listing all of those scriptures, for they are listed in a later chapter of this book.

If a pastor chooses to ignore these biblical truths and consequently does not have faith in the area of healing, he will look for every opportunity to justify sickness and disease. For example, he will refer to "Paul's thorn in the flesh" as a sickness or disease, even though scripture clearly states that it was a demon sent to buffet him, not make him sick. *And lest I should be exalted above measure through the abundance of the revelations, there was given to me a thorn in the flesh, the messenger of Satan to buffet me, lest I should be exalted above measure. For this thing I besought the Lord thrice, that it might depart from me. And he said unto me, My grace is sufficient for thee: for my strength is made perfect in weakness. Most gladly therefore will I rather glory in my infirmities, that the power of Christ may rest upon me.* (**2Corinthians 12:7-9**) The term, "thorn in the flesh" is the same term used to describe what the Israelites were to the Pharaoh of Egypt... with a modern translation meaning "pain in the rear." Just like a thorn in the flesh creates an irritation, so were the Israelites a major irritation to the Pharaoh.

Paul was performing many miracles and wonders by the power of the Holy Spirit and had many followers, obtaining fame and notoriety among the people. Even though Paul was giving God the credit and the glory, it would be very easy, as it is today for other men of God, for him to become puffed up and proud. This demon was allowed to basically keep him humble and not get caught up in the works of his ministry and the many revelations he received fro God, but rather to keep his eyes on the goal and the prize set before him. Paul was persecuted by being thrown into prison, whipped, stoned, harassed, put in stocks, driven out-of-town, ship- wrecked, snake bitten and ridiculed, all of which played a big part in preventing Paul from becoming proud and puffed up. For an in-depth study go to Tom Brown's article, "Paul's Thorn" at http://www.beautifulfeetoutreach.com or http://www.awmi. net "Paul's Thorn" by Andrew Wommack. *It is appointed for men to die once, but after this the judgment.* **Hebrews 9:27** It does not say, it is appointed for men to **get sick** and die.

Satan is <u>the great con artist</u>, as we saw when he tried to convince Eve that she and Adam "shall not surely die" as God warned. He also came to Jesus at the end of His 40-day fast and tried to get Him to turn stones into bread, to jump off a high place and to bow down and worship Him to gain the world. So it is not surprising that Satan tried to trick God into stretching forth His hand and destroying everything that Job owned. When Satan suggested this to God, God did not even bother responding to Satan or dignifying him with an answer. Now, if Matthew Henry and others too numerous to mention can twist the scripture with conjecture to warp or mold the story into meaning what they want it to mean, or take it in a direction they want it to go, then why can't I give it my best shot, and put words into God's mouth?

(Job 1:8) *So Satan answered the LORD and said, "Does Job fear God for nothing? Have You not made a hedge around him, around his household, and around all that he has on every side? You have blessed the work of his hands, and his possessions have increased in the land. But now, stretch out Your hand and touch all that he has, and he will surely curse You to Your face!"*
Maybe God replied:

"Satan, didn't you just hear me tell you that *'there is none like him in the whole earth, a perfect and an upright man, one that fears God, and shuns evil'*? First of all, I would not do such a thing to one of my children who is perfect and upright, fears me and turns from evil. I'm not like you! I do not have to prove anything to you, and you have to obey My laws and can only do what I allow you to do. I have set my laws into place and as long as Job is obeying them, you have no authority to interfere with his life. If Job chooses by his free will to disobey Me, then and only then can you kill, steal or destroy."

God may have continued as follows: "Notice, Satan, that even though Job is saying things about me that are not true, that is not a sin. He is not breaking any laws. He is not sinning with his lips. He is, however, operating in fear because he is offering up sacrifices to me for his children who are living in sin. Fear is your territory and you can operate there by the words of Job's mouth. He has just opened up to you all that he has by fearing he will lose it. You are asking me to stretch forth my hand and touch everything he has... *Behold Satan everything he has is in your power, only you have no authority to touch his flesh* (yet)."

[**Later**] Okay, Satan, you just destroyed everything Job owns because his fear and fear-filled words allowed you access. Now look, Satan, Job is still worshipping and praising Me despite the fact he actually believes I just destroyed everything he owns, plus his family. But look, Satan, he still praises Me anyway, "*The Lord gives and the Lord takes away, blessed be the name of the Lord*" He doesn't realize you are the one killing, stealing and destroying. I know I reminded you earlier that you did not have the right to touch Job's flesh, and now you are trying to get me to put forth my hand and touch his flesh, saying, if I do he will curse me to my face. Well I've got news for you, Satan, Job is still perfect and upright and fears me and shuns evil, even though he is giving me credit for all your evil deeds.

[**Later**] Well Satan, do you hear what Job is saying now about me after you wreaked havoc on him? He is not sinning with his lips or cursing me, but he is now again operating in fear. He just said that the thing he feared would happen has happened, and the thing he was afraid would come upon him has come upon him. Fear opens up the door for you to operate, Satan, and you know that; so why are you trying to get ME to touch his flesh? *Behold Satan, he is in YOUR power, but don't take his life.*

Listen to what he is saying to his wife when she told him to curse Me and die. He said, *"Shouldn't we receive both good and evil from God?"* We have a situation now, said God. Job is starting to lose patience, the pain and suffering that you caused, along with his three friends insisting that he must have sinned against me and needs to repent, is taking its toll. Plus, he is starting to feel self-righteous and he is now demanding that I give an account for the suffering he thinks I am inflicting on him. He is now starting to realize that maybe it is the words of his mouth getting him into trouble. Watch, Satan, Job will soon repent for his holier-than-thou, self-righteous attitude. All the negative words he has been speaking towards Me I could forgive him and restore everything you have taken from him, Satan. Plus, I shall restore back to him two-fold and make his friends repent and ask his forgiveness and require that they ask Job to offer up burnt offerings to me for what they accused Job of doing.

There you have it! If others can conjecture, so can I. However, I would suggest that my supposition is more in line with the true nature and character of God.

As I was finishing up this manuscript I decided to try and find and advocate on the internet who believes as I do: that God did not allow Satan to test Job, nor did God test Job using Satan as His tool, but rather Job himself gave Satan permission to do what he did to him by the words of his own mouth. In my search, I discovered several startling facts. I Googled *Job's test* and discovered thirty-three million web entries on the topic of God testing Job! My need to write this book has been reinforced! After hours of searching I could not find one person with my point of view; however, I found dozens of non-believers stating that Christians are feeble-minded, ignorant lemmings following each other off a cliff, and how could anyone serve a God that would torture and brutalize a servant of His that He considered perfect, upright, God-fearing and shuns evil?

Funny thing, I've been asking the very same question for well over two years now. I have been listening to a local pastor's nationally syndicated radio program for several months here in San Diego and have been truly blessed by his preaching. This man, beyond any doubt, is being mightily used by God in his ministry. I did notice that I have not heard him preach a message on divine healing or prosperity. (I'm not referring to the "name it and claim it," "blab it and grab it" ministries.)

On this particular day I was drawn to one of his many interesting story illustrations. He was telling about some shepherds in Ireland who one year experienced an unseasonably cold fall, and it came about during the calving season. The ewes were leaving the barn in the morning with their nursing newborns in tow and would venture some distance into the neighboring meadows. As the sun set, the temperature would plunge to freezing. Because the ewes had thick, wool coats, they would not realize the imminent danger to their babies, who would perish before reaching the warmth of the barn. The growing losses were felt by all the neighboring farms until one enterprising shepherd shaved the top of his ewes' heads so they would feel the cold immediately and hightail it to the barn, saving their babies from sure death. I thought, what a great story, until he began explaining that we are the sheep and God is the shepherd that will sometimes shave our heads to get us to come to Him in the barn. Then he added that God will sometimes allow Satan to put sickness on us to bring us to him or teach us a lesson.

That brings me to the next startling discovery on the internet that same day. I ran across an article on a pastor who was talking about how God used Satan to afflict Job to teach him a lesson. Then, bingo! The article went on to explain that this pastor "has been fighting cancer for five years." Notice the words, HE has been fighting cancer...however, the fight is not HIS. Jesus won the fight on the cross and said *"It is finished."* He took our sickness, disease and infirmities on the cross and we receive the free GIFT of healing the same way we receive the free GIFT of salvation, by **faith**. I have never heard this pastor preach that! Maybe because he does not truly believe it? Think about it... if this same man believes that God allowed Satan to afflict Job to teach him a lesson and he believes it is God's will, how could he possibly pray for a healing? If he did, he would be praying against God's will for his life and so would everyone else that prayed for him. *My people are destroyed for a lack of knowledge.* **Hosea 4:6** Jesus taught his disciples how to pray, *Our Father which art in heaven, hallowed be thy name, thy kingdom come, thy will be done* — WHERE? On earth as it is in heaven! What is God's will for us here on earth? The same as it is in heaven! Are there sickness, disease and infirmities in heaven? No!

The next startling discovery on the internet under "Job's test" was the movie "The Wager" which was released on December 31, 2007 starring Randy Travis, Nancy Stafford, Jude Ciccolella, Nancy Valen, Candace Cameron Bure, and Bronson Pinchot. The distributor is Pure Flix Entertainment, the director is Judson Pearce Morgan, the executive producers are Steve Seabury and Milton Mabry, the producers are Michael Scott, Russell Wolfe, David A.R. White, and Elizabeth Travis, the writer is Judson Pearce Morgan. Here is a brief summary:

THE WAGER is a modern day Story of Job about a successful actor who finds himself fighting for his life and his faith in a supernatural wager between God and Satan. There are a couple of bumps in the script, but THE WAGER is a well-produced, well-acted, captivating drama with a very strong Christian worldview.

Synopsis:

THE WAGER is a modern day Story of Job. Michael Steele, played by country music star Randy Travis, is up for an Academy Award, but his wife is tired of his job coming first, so she walks out on him. He then hears a radio preacher, John Hagee, who asks, what if there was a wager between God and Satan where you lost everything and yet had to live the Beatitudes in extreme circumstances?

Within a few short hours, Michael loses everything. The tabloid vultures accuse him of adultery and even worse. His career crashes. Michael begins to see signs of the Beatitudes on the sides of buses and in the hands of homeless people, but when he tries to live them, he can't do it. He even ends up slugging one tabloid reporter.

Michael's sister works at a ministry called The Dream Center, which helps the most broken of people. He asks her how he can live the Beatitudes. She says, you can't, you need Jesus Christ. Then, she dies, and Michael needs a miracle.

I saw the trailer, and read the summary and review and it sounds like a great movie. Travis and Stafford are two of my favorite actors. If that's not enough, Pastor John Hagee is one of my favorite mentors. I have his incredible series on the Jewish Feasts and on the Lord's Prayer. In addition,

I praise his efforts and financial support for the nation of Israel.

What is sad, though, is that Pastor Hagee is supporting and endorsing this movie, appearing in the movie to espouse the view that God allowed Satan to beat up on His perfect, upright, God-fearing, evil-shunning servant Job. What concerns me the most is the title of the movie, "THE WAGER."

The title presumes that the truth and premise of the story of the Book of Job was that God made a wager with Satan. First of all, why would God need to do that? He knows what Job is capable of doing or how he might hold up under pressure. God does not need to prove anything to Satan. The only thing God said to Satan was to make an observation that, *behold, Satan, everything he has is in your power..."*

How can anyone take that statement of observation, not permission, and turn it into a diabolical wager using a "perfect, upright, God-fearing, evil-shunning servant of God?" Yes, Satan was trying to get God to strike Job, but he refused! Where is the wager? Job brought all of his grief and suffering upon himself by running his mouth and making negative comments. Exactly like the modern day Job character Michael Steele, played by Randy Travis: "I can't do this," "Our marriage isn't going to make it," "I can't take this anymore"... one negative comment after another. The entire book of Job was about how our words produce consequences, positive or negative. You decide!

So now we are going to take one of the most important and most misunderstood books of the Bible, twist it into a modern-day knot, and dump it on an unsuspecting, non-discerning public. Non-believers already have a hard time understanding why God supposedly allows bad things to happen to "good" people. Now you want these same confused people to think that God not only ignores injustice, but actually participates in it, making wagers with the devil, betting whether or not the innocent, perfect, upright servants can hold up under the persistent onslaught of mayhem and torture. It is not surprising that so many non-believers have serious questions about the fairness, justice, mercy, grace and love of God when the majority of preachers and pastors interpret God's involvement in the life of Job to be nothing more than a wager between God and His adversary, the Devil — waiting to see whether or not he will buckle under grave, unwarranted hardship, loss, heartache and physical pain.

Many prominent Bible scholars refer to the book of Job as a lesson on "how to suffer." I beg to differ! It is a perfect manual to learn how to avoid unnecessary suffering, including these concepts:

1. Remember the **power of words** and choose them wisely, for they have the ability to create or destroy, bless or curse, create life or death; the tongue!
2. **Seek first the kingdom of God**, and his righteousness; and all these things shall be added unto you.
3. If we **confess our sins**, he is faithful and just to forgive us our sins, and to cleanse us from all unrighteousness.
4. For **God hath not given us the spirit of fear**; but of power, and of love, and of a sound mind.
5. He **shall not be afraid** of evil tidings: his **heart is fixed, trusting in the LORD.**
6. **Repent** and turn yourselves from all your transgressions; so iniquity shall not be your ruin.
7. **Humble yourselves in the sight of the Lord** and he shall lift you up. And whosoever shall exalt himself shall be abased; and **he that shall humble himself shall be exalted.**
8. The Lord has come that you might have an abundant life and Satan has come to kill, steal and destroy.

9. If there is any killing, stealing or destroying going on in your life, **don't blame God as Job did, blame Satan** and realize that the **words of your mouth and the condition of your heart** are what **gave him the permission,** not God!

10. For the LORD God is a sun and shield: the LORD will give grace and glory: **no good thing will he withhold from them that walk uprightly.**

CHAPTER 2

The Origin of Job's Problems

To best explain why bad things happen to "so-called good people," I need to start at the Garden of Eden, right after the only living God created heaven and earth. The Lord God commanded Adam, saying that of every tree of the garden he may eat freely, except for the tree of the *knowledge of good and evil*; and if he do eat from it he would surely die. God then created Eve as a mate for Adam, and then a fourth entity appears in the garden.

Genesis 3: *Now the serpent was more cunning than any beast of the field which the Lord God had made. And he said unto the woman, "has God said you shall not eat of every tree of the garden?" And the woman said to the serpent, "we may eat of the fruit of the trees of the garden: but of the fruit of the tree which is in the midst of the garden God has said, you shall not eat of it, neither shall you touch it or you will die." And the serpent said to the woman, "you shall not surely die: for God knows that in the day you eat of it, then your eyes shall be opened, and you shall be as gods, knowing good and evil." And when the woman saw that the tree was good for food, and that it was pleasant to the eyes and a treat to be desired to make one wise, she took of the fruit and ate it and gave some to her husband that he did eat it.*

27

Now notice the results of the words and actions of Adam, Eve and the Serpent:

And the eyes of them both were opened and they knew that they were naked: and they sewed fig leaves together and made themselves aprons. And they heard the voice of the Lord God walking in the garden in the cool of the day: Adam and his wife hid themselves from the presence of the Lord God among the trees of the garden. And the Lord God called unto Adam and said to him, "where are you?" And he said, "I heard your voice in the garden and I was afraid because I was naked and I hid myself. And God said, "who told you that you were naked? Have you eaten from the tree that I commanded you not to eat from?"

And the man said, the woman whom you gave to be with me she gave me of the tree and I did eat. Unto the woman He said, I will greatly multiply your sorrow and your conception; in sorrow you shall bring forth children; and your desire shall be to your husband and he shall rule over you. And unto Adam said, because you have hearkened unto the voice of your wife and have eaten of the tree of which I commanded you saying you shall not eat of it: **cursed is the ground for your sake; in sorrow show you eat of it all the days of your life; thorns also thistles will bring forth to you and you shall eat the herb; and in the sweat of your face shall you eat bread until you return to the ground; from out of there were you taken: from dust thou art and unto dust shall you return.**

And the Lord said behold, and now the man has become as one of us, to know good and evil; and now, lest he put forth his hand and take also of the **Tree of Life***, and eat, and live forever: therefore the Lord God sent him forth from the garden of Eden till the ground from where he was taken. So he drove out the man; and he placed at the east of the Garden of Eden, cherubims and a flaming sword which turned every way to keep the way of the tree of life.*

There you have it! Why bad things happen... It's called **sin**, a corrupt and fallen world; the result of man's **disobedience** and **rebellion** towards God.

Genesis 6:11-12 *The earth was **corrupt** before God, and the earth was filled with violence. And God looked upon the earth, and, behold, it was **corrupt**; for all flesh had corrupted his way upon the earth.*

Psalms 14:1 *The fool hath said in his heart, [There is] no God. They are **corrupt**, they have done abominable works, there is none that doeth good.*

John 1:29 *The next day John saw Jesus coming unto him, and said, Behold the Lamb of God, which takes away the **sin** of the world.*

Romans 3:9 *What then? Are we better than they? No, in no way: for we have before proved both Jews and Gentiles, that they are all under **sin**.*

Romans 3:20 *Therefore by the deeds of the law there shall no flesh be justified in his sight: for by the law of God comes the knowledge of **sin**.*

Romans 5:12 *Wherefore, as by one man [Adam] **sin** entered into the world, and death by **sin**; and so death passed upon all men, for that all have sinned.*

Romans 6:23 *For the wages of **sin** is death; but the gift of God is eternal life through Jesus Christ our Lord.*

1John 1:8 *If we say that we have no **sin**, we deceive ourselves, and the truth is not in us.*

1John 3:8 *He that commits **sin** is of the devil; for the devil has sinned from the beginning. For this purpose the Son of God was manifested [born of a virgin], that he might destroy the works of the devil.*

Why did God place the *Tree of Knowledge of good and evil* in the garden? God's main purpose was to allow man to have a choice between right and wrong or Holy and Evil. Without these choices, man would be nothing more than a robot, programmed to do only what the Creator wanted. If you were God, would you create a being that had no choice but to honor, love and worship you? Of course not! If there are laws and rules to govern one's behavior, shouldn't there also be consequences for your free choices?

Why is it, then, that when we make a choice that breaks one of God's laws, we blame Him for the consequences that we suffer? You expect to suffer the consequences when breaking one of God's laws of nature such as gravity; then why wouldn't you expect similar results from breaking God's spiritual or moral laws? What excuse do people have that have never read the Bible? God says none!

Romans 1:18-32 *The wrath of God is being revealed from heaven against all the godlessness and wickedness of men who suppress the truth by their wickedness, since what may be known about God is plain to them, because God has made it plain to them. For since the creation of the world God's invisible qualities—his eternal power and divine nature—have been clearly seen, being understood from what has been made, so that men are without excuse. For although they knew God, they neither glorified him as God nor gave thanks to him, but their thinking became futile and their foolish hearts were darkened. Although they claimed to be wise, they became fools and exchanged the glory of the immortal God for images made to look like mortal man and birds and animals and reptiles. Therefore God gave them over in the sinful desires of their hearts to sexual impurity for the degrading of their bodies with one another. They exchanged the truth of God for a lie, and worshiped and served created things rather than the Creator—who is forever praised. Because of this, God gave them over to shameful lusts. Even their women exchanged natural relations for unnatural ones. In the same way the men also abandoned natural relations with women and were inflamed with lust for one another. Men committed indecent acts with other* *men, and received in themselves the due penalty for their perversion. Furthermore, since they did not think it worthwhile to retain the knowledge of God, he gave them over to a depraved mind; to do what ought not to be done. They have become filled with every kind of wickedness, evil, greed and depravity. They are full of envy, murder, strife, deceit and malice. They are gossips, slanderers, God-haters, insolent, arrogant and boastful; they invent ways of doing evil; they disobey their parents; they are senseless, faithless, heartless, and ruthless. Although they know God's righteous decree that those who do such things deserve death, they not only continue to do these very things but also approve of those who practice them.*

You may never have read the Bible, yet you know instinctively when you have broken one of God's laws. Your conscience tells you so. God's laws are (**II Corinthians 3:3**)... *written not with ink but with the Spirit of the living God, not on tablets of stone but on tablets of human hearts.* When we sin by breaking God's laws, our conscience tells us so. The word *conscience* is made up of two Latin words, the first word *con*, means <u>with</u>. The second word, science means, <u>knowledge</u>. When you put the two together, it means, <u>with knowledge</u>. So when you say or do something that you know to be wrong, you do it with knowledge (con-science) that it is sin or displeasing your Creator, God. His laws have been written on every human heart.

CHAPTER 3

The Power of Our Words

How important is our tougue? One obvious answer to this question would be, if it wasn't for our tongues we would not be able to communicate by forming and enunciating our words. The key to unlocking the sources, causes and reasons for Job's suffering and great loss can be found in the hidden truth about the "power of the tongue." The recorded history of human success and failure can be traced back to the power of words through the tongue.

For you to completely understand how God intended our tongues to be used, we must go back to the very beginning.

In the beginning, God created the heavens and the earth and everything that is on it, under it, and above it. What is written about how God actually created everything? Well, the Bible records in **Genesis 1:3** *And God said, Let there be light: and there was light.* **Genesis 1:6** *And God said, Let there be a firmament in the midst of the waters, and let it divide the waters from the waters.* **Genesis 1:9** *And God said, Let the waters under the heaven be gathered together unto one place, and let the dry land appear: and it was so.* **Genesis 1:11** *And God said, Let the earth bring forth grass, the herb yielding seed, and the fruit tree yielding fruit after his kind, whose seed is in itself, upon the earth: and it was* *so*. **Genesis 1:14** *And God said, Let there be lights in the firmament of the heaven to divide the day from the night; and let them be for signs, and for seasons, and for days, and years.* **Genesis 1:20** And *God said, Let the waters bring forth abundantly the moving creature that has life, and fowl that may fly above the earth in the open firmament of heaven.* **Genesis 1:20** *And God said, Let the waters bring forth abundantly the moving creature that has life, and fowl that may fly above the earth in the open firmament of heaven.* **Genesis 1:26** And *God said, Let us make man in our image, after our likeness: and let them have dominion over the fish of the sea, and over the fowl of the air, and over the cattle, and over all the earth, and over every creeping thing that creeps upon the earth.* What is the key word in the process of God's act of creating? SAID! He **spoke** everything into existence by the power of **His Words!** God and **His Word** are the same. **John 1:1** *In the beginning was the **Word**, and the **Word** was with God, and the **Word was God**.* [This verse has been translated the same in all Bible translations with the exception of the Jehovah Witnesses.][1]

God used **words to create everything**. Everything was formed and made by God **speaking** everything into existence by the use of **words**. Jesus came to earth not only to save us from our sin and eternal death, but He also was here to show us the character and nature of the Father God and the power contained in our own words. Jesus said, *if you see me, you have seen the Father, the Father and I are one*. If He was here to show us the true nature of God the Father and how

---

[1] This "cult," which publishes the NEW WORLD TRANSLATION Bible, mistranslates this passage (in addition to other passages) in a shocking way, e.g., "Originally the Word was, and the Word was with God, and the Word was **a** god." Why did they add **a** and change the capital **G** to a little **g** in god? They did it to justify their perverted gospel that we all will someday be gods as God is God! See http://www.towerwatch.com.

He expects us to live our lives, we will have to ask, what did we learn from Jesus?

Jesus said, *I have come that you might have life and have it more abundantly, and the thief* [Satan] *comes to steal, kill and destroy.* So if there is any killing, stealing, or destroying going on, according to Jesus, who's doing it? Is cancer or sickness the abundant life? Is poverty or lack the abundant life? What is God's will in the area of sickness and/or poverty?

Well, let's take a look at the model prayer that Jesus taught his disciples to pray. *Our Father, who art in heaven, hallowed be thy name, thy kingdom come, thy will be done, on earth as it is*—where? In heaven! Thy will be done on earth as it is in heaven. What is God's will on earth? The same as it is in heaven! Is there cancer in heaven? Is there sickness or lack or poverty in heaven? Keep in mind, this is a <u>model prayer</u> that Jesus taught his disciples to pray. So the next time you question whether or not sickness in your body is from God, you know the answer, no!

Once we understand where sickness comes from, we can understand why we are able to get rid of it! God clearly reveals that both death and sickness originated with sin and are being spread by Satan. **Ephesians 2:2** *Wherein in time past you walked according to the course of this world, according to the prince of <u>the power of the air</u>, the spirit that now works in the children of disobedience.* **Romans 5:12-21** *Wherefore, as by one man sin entered into the world, and death by sin; and so death passed upon all men, for that all have sinned.* Remember, Jesus showed us the true nature of our Heavenly Father. God spoke everything into existence with words and Jesus did the same using words. Everything Jesus did, He did by faith in God. Jesus said in **John 5:30** *I can of mine own self do nothing: as I hear, I judge: and my judgment is just; because I seek not mine own will, but the will of the Father which has sent me.* **John 14:12** *Verily,*

verily, I say unto you, He that believeth on me, the works that I do shall he do also; and greater works than these shall he do; because I go unto my Father. **Mark 11:23** *For verily I say unto you, That whosoever* **shall say** *unto this mountain, Be removed, and be cast into the sea; and <u>shall not doubt in his heart</u>, but* **shall believe** *that those things which he* **says** *shall come to pass; he shall have whatsoever he* **says***.* You **shall have** whatsoever you say!

Most doctors believe that, only they don't refer to it as faith, they call it psychosomatic, defined as: (sī'kō-sō-măt'ĭk) 1. Of or relating to a disorder having physical symptoms but originating from mental or emotional causes. 2. Relating to or concerned with the influence of the mind on the body, and the body on the mind, especially with respect to disease: psychosomatic illness. (Wikipedia.com) A patient literally **talks** himself into an illness. Have you ever gotten cold, chilled and wet and **thought** to yourself, "I'll probably catch a cold," and even spoken out loud to whoever was around to hear? And lo and behold, you got one and then commenced to **tell** everyone about it, reinforcing the fact that you definitely had a cold. How many commercials for Nyquil T.M. or Vicks T.M. have you heard someone **say**, "It's cold and flu season, you need to stock up on such and such medicine..." or "...ask your doctor if *this* is right for you." What do you do the next time you see Nyquil T.M. or Vicks T.M. in the store? The commercial actor telling you to stock up was dressed up like a what? A doctor or nurse, of course. Why? Because most people look to doctors as gods to work miracles in the area of healing. Here is an account of a woman in the Bible who had heard of Jesus and believed he could heal her. **Luke 8:43-44** *And a woman having an issue of blood <u>twelve years</u>, which had spent all her living upon physicians, neither could any of them heal her, came behind Jesus, and touched the border of His garment: and immediately her issue of blood* *stopped.* Does psychosomatic conditioning and faith work the same way?

Isaiah 53:5 *But he was wounded for our transgressions, he was bruised for our iniquities: the chastisement of our peace was upon him; and with his stripes we are healed.* When Adam and Eve sinned they brought a curse upon the earth and all mankind. **Sickness is a curse,** and Jesus not only died for our sins, **He died for our sickness; he took both our sin and sickness upon the cross... and with His stripes we are healed!** With the **words of your mouth** (tongue) you can confess sickness or health, receive curses or blessings. You have a free will and the choice is yours. Jesus warned his disciples continuously about the **power of the tongue** and the consequences of our **words.** Jesus said in **James 3:5-6,** *Even so, the **tongue** is a little member, and **boasts** great things. Behold how great a matter a little fire kindles! And the **tongue** is a fire, a world of iniquity: so is the **tongue** among our members, that it defiles the whole body, and sets on fire the course of nature; and it is set on fire of hell. But no man can tame the **tongue; it is an unruly evil, full of deadly poison.***

Did you know that words can create or destroy? **Matthew 21:19-22** *And when he saw a fig tree in the way, he came to it, and found nothing thereon, but leaves only, and **said** unto it, Let no fruit grow on you henceforward forever. And presently the fig tree withered away. And when the disciples saw it, they marveled, saying, how soon is the fig tree withered away! Jesus answered and said unto them, Verily I say unto you, If you have faith, **and doubt not,** you shall not only do this which is done to the fig tree, for verily I say unto you, That whosoever shall **say** unto this mountain, Be removed, and be cast into the sea; and **shall not doubt in his heart, but shall believe** that those things which he says shall come to pass; he shall have whatsoever he **says.** This... you shall have, whatsoever things you **say.*** **John 14:13** *And* *whatsoever you shall **ask** in my name, that will I do, that the Father may be glorified in the Son.*

How did Jesus wither the fig tree? He **spoke** to it! How did He calm the storm? He **spoke** to it, **saying** *"peace be still."* How did he raise Lazarus from the dead? He **spoke** to him **saying,** *Lazarus, come forth*! How did he cast out devils? He **spoke** to them! How did he restore the blind man's sight? He simply **said,** *receive your sight.* And to the man who was crippled from birth, he **said,** *take up your bed and walk.*

Because **words have power**, Jesus warned us to pick our **words** carefully. He said in **Philippians 4:8** *Finally, brethren, whatsoever things are true, whatsoever things are honest, whatsoever things are just, whatsoever things are pure, whatsoever things are lovely, whatsoever things are of good report; if there be any virtue, and if there be any praise, **think** on these things.* And **Luke 6:45** *A good man out of the good treasure of his heart brings forth that which is good; and an evil man out of the evil treasure of his heart brings forth that which is evil: for out of the abundance of the heart his mouth **speaks**.* **James 3:11-12** *Does a fountain send forth at the same place sweet water and bitter? Can the fig tree, my brethren, bear olive berries? Either a vine, figs? So can no fountain both yield salt water and fresh.*

How do you learn to control your **tongue**? To control your **tongue,** you must first learn to control your mind. The key for controlling your **words** is first learning to control right and wrong thinking. **Proverbs 23:7** *As a man thinks in his heart, so is he.* In other words, a man **is** what he thinks. This is one of God's most important laws. Man-made laws can be **changed;** many of man's laws have loopholes, allowing them to be manipulated. God's laws are based on spiritual principles and they cannot be changed or broken. You cannot manipulate, *"whatsoever a man sows, that you shall also reap."* Plus you can never break **God's laws** without corresponding results. What were the consequences of Adam's sin in the Garden of Eden? If you gossip about someone, you will become the target of someone else's gossip. If you judge someone, you will be judged yourself. Laws of nature and the laws of physics are at all times dependable. (For example, for every action there is an equal and opposite reaction. At 32° Fahrenheit, water will freeze and at 212° it will boil.) God's laws and principles can be used to achieve a positive or negative result. The sooner we accept that fact, the better.

What is the origin of our **thoughts**? There are basically three sources: The first: **thoughts** originate through our five senses. Everything you have learned throughout your life has come through your sense of sight, hearing, smell, touch or taste. Our senses can trigger thoughts based upon experiences from the past. A sound or smell can trigger a childhood memory, either good or bad. The taste of the food can trigger memories from long ago.

The second source of **thoughts** is from God, placed in our mind or heart by the Holy Spirit. God speaks to your spirit and your spirit, in turn, speaks to your mind. **Romans 12:2** *And be not conformed to this world: but be transformed by the renewing of your mind, that you may prove what is the good, acceptable, and perfect will of God.*

The third source of **thoughts** can come from Satan, who will bombard your mind with **thoughts** of fear, failure, lack, worry, lust, hatred, superiority, or inferiority—the list goes on. The Bible states that Satan put the **thought** of betraying Jesus into Judas's mind. Fortunately, Satan cannot read your mind; he can only attack it with evil **thoughts**. The safest way of discerning whether a **thought** is from God or from Satan is to renew your mind daily with the **Word of God**! Your mind is like a computer: what you feed into it is the only information you have to work with. "Garbage in, garbage out."

Your computer or brain has been programmed throughout your life: by the things we've learned in school, from the people we hang around, television, movies, radio, or by our circumstances and experiences—both good and bad. Reprogramming your mind is not like reprogramming a computer. With a computer you can delete unwanted information, but with your mind all **thoughts** remain on one "hard drive." Reprogramming your mind would be like un-popping popcorn. The good news is, **God's Word** has the ability to lessen the effects that negative or bad **thoughts** have on our minds. You simply learn to give **God's Word** priority over your **thoughts** and choose **His Word** to influence your choice of **words**. The more of **God's Word** you memorize, the easier it will be to accept or reject **thoughts** according to what God's Word says. **2Timothy 2:15** *Study to show yourself approved unto God, a workman that needs not to be ashamed, rightly dividing the word of truth.* **2Corinthians 10:5** says*: Casting down imaginations, and every high thing that exalts itself against the knowledge of God, and **bringing into captivity every thought** to the obedience of Christ.*

What does that mean? Let's say you were worrying about having clothes to wear or food to eat and your mind was plagued by these **thoughts**, whether put there by Satan or **thoughts** of your own. Yet God has told us in His Word, **Philippians 4:19** *God shall supply all your need according to His riches in glory by Christ Jesus.* So which **thought** do you dwell on, supply or lack? The more you meditate and dwell on **God's Word,** the more you will think like God thinks. The Bible tells us in **I Corinthians 2:16** *We have the mind of Christ.* If you desire to know who God is, you can find the answers in **His Word.**

Many people think that God is too far above us and we will never know why He operates the way He does. You may have heard this phrase before: "God works in strange and mysterious ways His wonders to perform." Many people think that it is a verse from the Bible, **but it is not. Ephesians1:9** says, *Having made known unto us the mystery of His will.*

True power, freedom, peace, joy, security, and happiness come from truly knowing God through His Son Jesus Christ, and by **His Word.** God will not leave you in the dark. **Psalm 119:105** says, *Thy word is a lamp unto my feet and a light unto my path.* **Proverbs 3:5-6** *Trust in the Lord with all your heart, and do not lean on your own understanding. In all your ways acknowledge Him, and He will make straight your paths.* As we pass through life, we have many decisions to make. Wouldn't it be best if we used God's wisdom rather than our own to make them? Most people simply rely on past experience, the experiences of others, or sometimes even the advice of a palm reader, psychic, or horoscope to make their decisions.

What happens if we do not cast down **thoughts** that are not from God and thoughts that exalt themselves above **God's Word?** Those thoughts, if we dwell on them long enough, can become **imaginations;** and **imaginations,** if not checked, can turn into **strongholds.** A thought is much easier to cast down than an **imagination,** and even more so with strongholds. You see a movie advertised on television which is rated R for graphic language, sex, nudity, violence. You continue to **think** about it, and you **think** about the rush you received from watching the previews. Soon, you start **imagining** yourself going to the movie and **imagining** the excitement you will experience from watching it. Now you feel you must see it, you have to see it, you will not be happy until you see it; it has now become a **stronghold.** Instead, you should have originally compared this thought to what **God's Word** says: **Philippians 4:8** *Finally, brethren, whatsoever things are true, whatsoever things are honest, whatsoever things are just, whatsoever things are pure, whatsoever things are lovely, whatsoever things are of good report; if there be any virtue, and if there be any praise, think on these things.* So ask yourself, was the movie true, honest, just, pure, lovely, a good report, virtuous, praiseworthy? If

41

not, then it is obviously not pleasing to God and therefore, by watching it, you would not be pleasing God either.

If you are truly living your life to please God and expecting the blessings of God by putting Him first in your life, then you should examine every **thought** that enters your mind, and determine if it lines up with **God's Word**. This is what is referred to as programming your mind with the **Word of God**. So before a negative **thought** can become an **imagination** and, in turn, a **stronghold** which can control your life, throw it out. If "stinkin–thinkin" has already resulted in a **stronghold** (habits or addictions), then go to **2 Corinthians 10:3-5** *For though we live in the world, we do not wage war as the world does. The weapons we fight with are not the weapons of the world. On the contrary, they have divine power to demolish **strongholds**. We demolish arguments and every pretension that sets itself up against the knowledge of God, and we take captive every **thought** to make it obedient to Christ.* Your **thoughts** will define you, making you who you are. Jesus has given you authority over your **thoughts**, but you have to exercise that authority, staying in authority by and as an act of your free will.

An **imagination** is a conscientious intent to act upon a **thought**. When you have submitted your will to the act, the **thought** has now become a **stronghold**. As an example, let's say you need to buy two batteries for your camera. At the store you make a shocking discovery, these are special batteries that cost seven dollars each. Once you get over the shock, you think, how can these batteries be that different from a dollar battery? You think, what a rip-off! You think, highway robbery! You think, that is totally out of line, no one should have to pay seven dollars for a battery. You think, but I really need these batteries and I only have ten dollars. Then you think, it sure would be easy to just slip these batteries in my pocket, and I can pay for them later the next time I am in this store. I can just tell them I forgot to pay. Then you think, that is a great solution! Then you think, that's not really stealing, if I intend to pay later. And you think, I don't have time to go to the bank or ATM for more cash. Then you think, I really don't have a choice, take them now and pay for them later, I promise, cross my heart and hope to die. Your thought has quickly become an imagination. No one is looking, and you slip the batteries into your pocket. Your thoughts have now become a stronghold, but what is worse, the next time you come into the store you conveniently forget about the overpriced, rip-off batteries. Now you're a thief, but a justified one! However, the good news is that, **1 John 1:9** *If we confess our sins, He is faithful and just to forgive us [our] sins, and to cleanse us from all unrighteousness.* That's the first step toward demolishing strongholds, confession and repentance; the second step is restitution, return or pay for the stolen items. Isn't it great! You can now feel clean, and fellowship has been restored with the Savior. **Colossians 3:15** *And let the peace of God rule in your hearts.*

Let all your **thoughts** become subject to that peace of God in your heart. If a **thought** does not rest well with the peace of God, then dismiss it. Our mind is a spiritual battleground where there are only two outcomes, victory or defeat. Most coaches of sports know this to be true, and spend a considerable amount of time attempting to program the athlete's mind. He chooses his **words** carefully so that they will promote positive **thoughts** to condition the mind of each player. All of their **thoughts** and the **words** of their **mouths** reflect and confess victory. The mind is a fertile soil for the seeds of both victory and defeat. The seeds of victory planted in your mind and watered with **words** of encouragement and exhortation produce the fruits of victory. These are the positive results using the same framework of **thoughts** becoming **imaginations,** resulting in strongholds. **Thoughts** of victory, resulting in imagining victory, culminating in a

stronghold of victory! **God's Word** is victory! *For God has not given you the spirit of fear, but of power, love, and a sound mind.*

You've heard the phrase, "mind over matter"; however, with true believers, the phrase is **"words [tongue]** over matter." Here Jesus describes gossip, **James 3:6** *And the* **tongue** *is a fire, a world of iniquity: so is the* **tongue** *among our members, that it defiles the whole body, and sets on fire the course of nature; and it is set on fire of hell.* The result of **God's Word** abiding in us: **John 15:7** *If you abide in me, and my* **words** *abide in you, you shall* **ask** *what you will, and it shall be done unto you.* **John 15:16** *You have not chosen me, but I have chosen you, and ordained you, that you should go and bring forth fruit, and that your fruit should remain: that whatsoever you shall* **ask** *of the Father in my name, he may give it you.* **Matthew 18:19** *Again I* **say** *unto you, that if two of you shall agree on earth as touching anything that they shall* **ask**, *it shall be done for them of my Father which is in heaven.*

Satan is very much aware of the power of words as a result of his many encounters with Jesus. After fasting for 40 days in the wilderness Satan came to Him and said in **Matthew 4:3** *And when the tempter came to Him, he said, "If you be the Son of God,* **command** *that these stones be made bread."* As you read in the Gospels, the many accounts of the miracles performed by Jesus were the results of His spoken words. And Jesus said, **John 14:12** *Verily, verily, I say unto you, He that believes on me, the works that I do shall he do also; and greater works than these shall he do; because I go unto my Father.* We can do what Jesus did, by faith, and through his resurrection power; and Satan knows it and is trying to do everything within his power to stop it. Satan's influence is everywhere. Check out some common clichés: I am **sick** to **death;** I am **sick** and **tired;** that scared me to **death;** when do we eat, **I'm starving;** you're going to catch your **death** of cold; you make me **sick;** I'm **dead** on my feet; they are a **pain in the neck**; well I'll be **damned**; they'll be the **death** of me. **Proverbs 18:21** *Death and life are in the power of the tongue.* **James 3:5-8** *Even so the tongue is a little member and boasts great things. See how great a forest a little fire kindles! And* **the tongue is a fire, a world of iniquity.** *The tongue is so set among our members that it defiles the whole body, and* **sets on fire the course of nature;** *and* **it is set on fire by hell.** *But* **no man can tame the tongue.** *It is an unruly evil,* **full of deadly poison.**

So what is the solution? **God's Word!** Model the prayers of David in **Psalms 34:13** *Keep your tongue from evil and your lips from speaking lies.* **Proverbs 4:24** *Put away perversity from your mouth; keep corrupt* **talk** *far from your lips.* **Proverbs 8:7** *My* **mouth** *speaks what is true, for* **my lips detest wickedness.** **Proverbs 10:32** *The* **lips** *of the righteous know what is fitting, but the* **mouth** *of the wicked only what is perverse.* **Proverbs 13:3** *He who* **guards his lips** *guards his life, but he who* **speaks** *rashly will come to ruin.* **Proverbs 17:28** *Even a fool is thought wise if he keeps silent, and discerning if he holds his tongue.* **Proverbs 18:7** *A fool's* **mouth** *is his undoing and his* **lips** *are a snare to his soul.*

Well, Jesus said it best, *for out of the abundance of the heart, the* **mouth speaks.** So when someone **speaks**, they are revealing what is in their heart. **Jeremiah 17:9** *The heart is deceitful above all things, and desperately wicked: who can know it?* Does it make sense that, for a person who never or rarely attends church or reads a Bible, the **Word of God** would not likely reside in their heart? **Hosea 4:6** says *"My people are destroyed for lack of knowledge."* Believing in God or in His Word requires faith. The Bible says, **Romans 10:17** *So then faith comes by hearing, and hearing by the word of God."* The more of the **Word of God** you know, the more you will know God and have faith in him. Would you have faith or trust in a stranger? No! However, if you had heard from a reliable source about the personality and nature of this person and discovered that he was honest, trustworthy, kind, loving, merciful, and gracious, it would be easy to put your **faith and trust in him.**

If it were true that if you put God first in your life, desired after Him, and kept His commandments, that whatever you **ask** of him **believing** that you would receive it, **would you be willing to do it?** Read the following and ask yourself, if what you're reading is **true**, would it be easier for you to cope with everyday stress and anxiety? These are the words of Jesus:

Matthew 6:19-34 *Lay not up for yourselves treasures upon earth, where moth and rust corrupt, and where thieves break through and steal: But lay up for yourselves treasures in heaven, where neither moth nor rust corrupt, and where thieves do not break through nor steal: For where your treasure is, there will your heart be also.*

The light of the body is the eye. If therefore your eye be clear, your whole body shall be full of light. But if your eye be evil, your whole body shall be full of darkness. If therefore the light that is in you be darkness, how great is that darkness!

No man can serve two masters: for either he will hate the one, and love the other; or else he will hold to the one, and despise the other. You cannot serve God and money. Therefore I say unto you, Take no thought for your life, what you shall eat, or what you shall drink; nor yet for your body, what you shall put on. Is not the life more than meat, and the body than raiment?

Behold the fowls of the air: for they sow not, neither do they reap, nor gather into barns; yet your heavenly Father feeds them. Are you not much better than they? Which of you by taking thought can add one cubit unto his stature [or one hour to your day]?

And why take thought for raiment? Consider the lilies of the field, how they grow; they toil not, neither do they spin: And yet I say unto you, that even Solomon in all his glory was not arrayed like one of these. Wherefore, if God so clothe the grass of the field, which today is, and tomorrow is cast into the oven, shall He not much more clothe you, O you of little faith?

Therefore take no thought, saying, what shall we eat? Or, what shall we drink? Or, how shall we be clothed? (For after all these things do the Gentiles seek), for your heavenly Father knows that you have need of all these things. But **seek first the kingdom of God, and His righteousness;** *and all these things shall be added to you.* And here is the good news: *Take therefore no thought for the morrow: for the morrow shall take thought for the things of itself. Sufficient unto the day is the evil thereof.*

By filling your mind with **God's Word** you now have a weapon to defeat Satan's attacks. When Satan says, "you are a loser and can do nothing right," you can reply, **Philippians 4:13** *I can do all things through Christ who strengthens me.* **1John 4:4** *He who is in you is greater than he* [Satan] *who is in the world.*

Jesus said: **John 14:14** *If you ask anything in My name, I will do it.* Was he a liar? No? Then **believe Him**, and put your **trust and faith in Him**, starting today!

Let's summarize: Jesus was speaking to the Pharisees in **Matthew 12:34** *Oh generation of vipers, how can you, being evil,* **speak** *good things?" (Out of the abundance of the heart the* **mouth speaks***.)* He went on to say that a good man, out of the good treasure of his heart, brings forth good things and the evil man, out of the evil treasures of his heart, brings forth evil things; you can't hide it or cover it up; if it's in your heart it's going to come out of your mouth. You might cover it up for a while, but the first time you become angry, frustrated, anxious, disappointed, hurt, betrayed, maligned, or things just aren't going your way, it is coming out of your mouth, from the abundance of your heart. **Matthew 12:36**

But I say unto you that every idle word that men shall **speak**, *they shall give account of in the Day of Judgment.... For by your* **words** *you will be justified, and by your* **words** *you will be condemned.* Our **words** can bless us or defile us. Jesus said that it is not that which goes into the mouth that defiles a man but rather that which **comes out of the mouth** which defiles him.

The Pharisees were pointing out to Jesus that some of His disciples did not wash their hands before eating. He later explained to His disciples the meaning of his statement in **Matthew 15:17-20** *...whatever enters into the mouth goes into the belly and is cast out into the draught* [sewer], *but those things which proceed* **out of the mouth**, *come forth from the heart and defile a man. For out of the heart proceed evil* **thoughts**, *murderers, adulteries, fornications, thefts, false witnesses, blasphemies; these are the things that defile a man. But to eat with unwashed hands defiles not a man.*

You are responsible for the results and consequences of your **words**. Your words are an extension of you. You are a spirit which lives in a body and your **words** are spirit and they have power to create or destroy. If you were to gossip about someone to several people, the effects of your **words** cannot be undone, for it is like taking a feather pillow, cutting a hole in it as you walk down the street shaking the feathers into the air. It would be impossible to retrieve those feathers, as it would be to retrieve the words that you spoke. That's why **God's Word** says in **2Corinthians 10:5** *Casting down imaginations, and every high thing that exalts itself against the knowledge of God, and bringing into captivity every* **thought** *to the obedience of Christ.*

Proverbs 4:20-24 *My son, give attention to My words; Incline your ear to My sayings. Do not let them depart from your eyes; keep them in the midst of your* **heart**; *for they are life to those who find them, and health to all their flesh. Keep your* **heart** *with all diligence, for out of it spring the* *issues of life. Put away from you a deceitful* **mouth**. *And put perverse* **lips** *far from you.* This is how you change your **heart**. *Incline your ear to My sayings, let them not depart from your eyes; keep them in the midst of your heart.* Where are they kept? In your **heart**! Where is your heart? When the Bible talks about your heart it is referring to the central part of the entire person. The Greek word for heart is "kardia" which is translated heart, or bowels and can refer to belly, inner man, hidden man, depending on the translation. What is the relationship between the heart, spirit, soul and body?

1Thessalonians 5:23 *May the God of peace Himself consecrate you through and through; and may your* **spirit and soul and body** *be kept complete so that you will be blameless at the coming of our Lord Jesus Christ.* The Scripture uses three of these in describing man, but does not use the word "heart." We find the following three words, spirit, soul, and body.

Greek	English	Meaning
Pneuma	Spirit	breath, wind, akin to pneĭn, to blow, breathe
Psuche	Soul	mind, as the center of thought, behavior, will, and emotions
Soma	Body	body, all the cells and tissues in the body considered collectively

In this verse "heart" is not mentioned, but it is used elsewhere referring to the core of the whole person. So what specifically does your "heart" include? Is it only the spirit or soul, or all three—spirit, soul and body? I suggest that spirit, soul and body encompass the whole man, and the heart is the central core of the mental and moral tapestry of the whole person. So what we think in our minds conditions the heart and the heart is a reflection of the whole person. As we feed on **God's Word** we are changing our heart which, in turn, regenerates our spirit, renews our mind, and transforms our body. **Romans 12:1-2** *I beseech you therefore, brethren, by the mercies of God, that you **present your bodies a living sacrifice, holy, acceptable unto God**, which is your reasonable service. And be not conformed to this world: but be transformed by the renewing of your mind that you may prove what is that good, and acceptable, and perfect will of God.*

Presenting your body to God as a living sacrifice requires submitting your will and emotions to the direction of the Holy Spirit. Your mind needs to be conformed to the **Word of God** so that it can cooperate with the leading of the Holy Spirit. God speaks to our spirit by his Holy Spirit which, in turn, directs the soul (mind, will, emotions); and the mind directs the body, which includes our mouth. Now we can be true ambassadors for God!

CHAPTER 4

Job Said but God Said

It is evident, after reading the book of Job, that he did not have a clue about the power of his words. However, after losing all that he owned, including his family, he intimated that perhaps his mouth may be partially to blame. **Job 6:30** *Is there any iniquity in my tongue? Cannot my taste discern perverse things?* By the time you reach the end of Chapter 37, Job has voiced 77 false charges against God. By the end of Jehovah's response in chapters 38 and 39, Job realizes that he may have stuck his foot in his mouth. Actually, he should have stuck a sock in it; however, he did the next best thing, he laid his hand over it. **Job 40:4-5** *Behold, I am vile; what shall I answer you? I will lay my hand upon my mouth. Once have I spoken; but I will not answer: yea, twice; but I will proceed no further.*

Was Job operating in fear? What difference would it make if he was? What harm can fear cause? Is fear a friend or foe? Is fear a positive or negative emotion? First, let's look at how fear is defined. According to the definition of **fear**, it can be both positive and negative. **1.** A distressing emotion aroused by impending danger, evil, pain, etc., whether the threat is real or imagined; the feeling or condition of being afraid. **2.** A reverential awe, especially toward God. Let's see what the Bible says about fear.

The Bible records man's first experience with fear as taking place in the Garden of Eden immediately following the event of Adam and Eve eating from the tree of the knowledge of good and evil. Prior to sinning, Adam and Eve had no knowledge of being naked; however, after disobeying God they had knowledge of their condition. They now had knowledge of good and evil resulting in awareness that they were naked. Knowing they had sinned and were naked, they feared what God might do and hid from him. God's laws are written on every man's heart, so that when we sin, we sin with the knowledge that we sinned. The type of fear that Adam experienced was a godly fear, stemming from a reverential awe.

What is required to believe in God? Quite simply, faith. We can't experience God with any of our senses, so consequently we have to accept Him by faith. Where does that faith come from? The Bible says, **Romans 10:17** *So then faith comes by hearing, and hearing by the word of God.* Quite simply, faith comes from hearing the Word of God; the more of the Word of God you have, the more you know about God. How can you put your trust and faith in someone you don't know? The more you get to know that person — that they are honest, trustworthy, loyal, kind, merciful, righteous, and loving — the more faith and trust you will have in them.

If you were not aware that Satan existed, and what kind of a monster he was, that he was out to kill, steal and destroy, and that he wanted you dead, then every time something bad happened to you, whom would you blame? If no one told you about the true nature of God as manifested in the person of Jesus Christ, that He had come "that you might have life and have it more abundantly," then who are you going to blame for all of the calamity, sickness, lack and pain in your life?

You would probably do as Job did, blame God for every-thing, giving him credit for both the good and the bad.

Most people have not read the Bible, let alone studied it. So what do they know about God? Case in point: Matthew Henry, with his library of Bible commentaries to his credit, is guilty of gross misrepresentation of the inspired Word of God! The portion of the word that is misrepresented deals with the Divine Nature of God. It warps His character and perverts the Justice of God, spinning a web of doubt and confusion on the very definition of His Grace and Mercy. The Greek and Hebrew translation of God's reply to Satan's request to destroy Job's possessions lines up accurately with the King James Translation, which is as follows: **Job 1:12** *And the LORD said unto Satan, Behold, all that he has is in your power; only upon himself put not forth your hand.* For God to state to Satan that: "Behold, all that he has is in your power" is not a permission to do anything, it is simple a statement of fact about the relationship between Job's possessions and Satan. Yet Mathew Henry has the brazen audacity to make the blanket statement of fact that "**God allowed him to do it...**" Rather than state the obvious, Satan proceeded with his plan of destruction and for some reason God did not stop him.

Did God give him permission or did the fear-motivated words of Job's own mouth give Satan permission? Is that a possibility? Was Jesus merely suggesting the possibility that the words of our mouth can bring blessings or cursing... bring life or death... create or destroy... tear down or build up... or did he emphatically warn us that spoken words will definitely produce results, either positive or negative? So was it obvious that when God stated that all that Job had was in Satan's power, He was giving him permission?

Obviously it was to Mathew Henry and thousands of other ministers, theologians and Bible scholars. In Henry's commentary he goes way beyond speculation; he dives right into fabrication with the embellishing touches of unquestionable probability. He goes on to twist the scripture by quoting **Job 1:12** this way: "All that he has is in your hand, make the trial as sharp as thou canst; do your worst at him." This distortion was followed with: "It is a **matter of wonder** that God should give Satan such **permission** as this, should **deliver** the soul of a turtle dove into the hand of the adversary, such a lamb to such a Lion. But He did it for **His own glory**, the **honor of Job**, the **explanation of providence** and the **encouragement of His afflicted people** in all ages." "Encouragement"?!! "His own Glory"?!! "The honor of Job"?!! "An explanation of providence"?!! You have got to be kidding! It is one thing to make a blanket statement of fact **that you know the mind of God** on a matter, but to blatantly and arrogantly add to scripture to **reinforce your point of view** or interpretation of an issue is absolutely INEXCUSABLE.

If you are one of those that have not read or studied the Bible, before you can understand the things of God, you must understand the meaning behind blood sacrifices.

Adam and Eve sinned through eating from the tree of the Knowledge of Good and Evil; they realized that they were naked through the act of sinning, and they tried to cover their nakedness using fig leaves. This act was symbolic of our attempt to cover up sin. This was figuratively and literally accomplished by God killing (sacrificing) an animal (shedding its blood) and using its hide to fashion an apron for each of them. This act was a type and shadow of things to come; in order for all sin to be covered, a sacrifice would be required (a price, fine, debt or penalty had to be paid). This event was a signpost pointing down through history to the ultimate sacrifice paid by Jesus Christ, the Son of God.

All of God's people were required to make a sacrifice for their sin. The type of sacrifice offered depended on the person's income status; it could range from a dove to a lamb or bull. In ancient Jerusalem, the priest would choose a spotless lamb once a year for sacrifice on the altar to cover the sins of the people for that **one year**. The blood of the Lamb was another signpost pointing to Jesus Christ, the spotless Lamb of God, whose blood will take away the sins of the world forever. This meant there was no more a requirement for blood sacrifice, for all one would need to do is repent and put their trust and faith in Jesus Christ for His forgiveness of sin. Jesus died in our place as the ultimate sacrifice for our sins, writing our names in the Lamb's Book of Life, securing our place in heaven.

Most Jews do not have a clue why the Israelites in Egypt, under the domination of the Pharaoh, were told by Moses to kill a lamb and place its blood above the doors and on the side posts. This procedure would protect them when the Angel of death flew over every household in Egypt. The firstborn of every household would die if the house did not display the lamb's blood on the door. This also was a type and shadow of the protection, healing and salvation that would come from the sacrifice and shed blood of the Lamb of God, "that would take away the sins of the world." Jesus said, *I am the way, the truth, and the life, and no man comes unto the Father but by me.* **John 3:16** *For God so loved the world, that he gave his only begotten son, that whosoever believes in him, shall not perish, but have everlasting life.*

Job definitely knew about the need for a sacrifice for sin, for the very first chapter of the book, **Job:4-5** says *...and his sons would go and feast in their houses, each on his appointed day, and would send and invite their three sisters to eat and drink with them. So it was, when the days of feasting had run their course, that Job would send and sanctify them, and he would rise early in the morning and offer burnt offerings according to the number of them all. For Job said, "It may be that my sons have sinned and cursed God in their hearts." This Job did regularly.* What was Job's motivation here, **fear** for his children's lives? Of course, and he proved it by his actions and his response to that fear. Fear is the opposite of faith. Satan operates in fear, God operates in faith! Why do you think that Jesus spent so much time talking about faith and its relationship to the words we speak and how the words that we do speak contain power to create or destroy? With our words we are giving power either to God or to Satan!

Hebrews 11:6 *But without faith it is impossible to please God: for he that comes to God must believe that He is, and that He is a rewarder of them that diligently seek Him.* Did God allow Satan to attack Job as a result of a wager between them? If God allowed Satan to destroy everything Job owned including his family, wasn't God indirectly doing it himself? Did God allow Satan to attack Job in order to test his loyalty to God? Did God allow Satan to attack Job to see if he could hold up under the pressure — or to teach him a lesson, or to bring him closer to God, or because he knew that Job could handle it and he should count it all joy that God would pick him to beat up on to use as an example for others? Unfortunately, most churches today subscribe to one of these premises. Is it any wonder that many people have a perverted, sick, twisted image of the Creator?

If you are one of those that answered yes to any of the previous questions, hopefully this book will give you renewed hope, faith and love in your heavenly Father.

We will begin with the meeting between Satan and God:

Job 1:6-12 *Now there was a day when the sons of God came to present themselves before the LORD, and Satan also came among them. And the LORD said to Satan, "From where do you come?" So Satan answered the LORD and said, "From going to and fro on the earth, and from walking back and forth on it." Then the LORD said to Satan, "Have you considered My servant Job, that there is none like him on the earth, a blameless and upright man, one who fears God and shuns evil?" So Satan answered the LORD and* *said, "Does Job fear God for nothing? Have You not made a hedge around him, around his household, and around all that he has on every side? You have blessed the work of his hands, and his possessions have increased in the land. But now, stretch out Your hand and touch all that he has, and he will surely curse You to Your face!" And the LORD said to Satan, "Behold, all that he has is in your power; only do not lay a hand on his person." So Satan went out from the presence of the LORD.*

Did God just give Satan permission to take Job's oxen, asses and kill his servants? To bring fire from the sky and burden of Job's sheep and more of his servants? Steal his camels and kill more of his servants? Kill his family and kill more servants? This is what most preachers, teachers, theologians and scholars ever since Mathew Henry have espoused.

In the same way Satan tried to trick Jesus into turning stones into bread, bowing down to worship him, and jumping off a high place to prove that he was God, Satan also tried to trick God into testing Job. Instead, God replied, *"Behold, all that he has is in your power; only do not lay a hand on his person."* That statement was not giving permission to Satan; God was merely pointing out a fact that all Job had was in his power. We should ask the question, why was everything that Job had in Satan's power? I did not hear God say, "I am placing everything that Job has in your power." All that he said was, *"Behold, all that he has is in your power."*

Was Job operating in faith or in fear? We already established that he was operating in fear prior to Satan's attack, by his perpetual offering of sacrifices for his wayward children. Does Job admit that he was operating in fear? Yes he does, in chapter 3, verse 25: *For the thing which I greatly feared is come upon me and that which I was afraid of is come unto me.* Fear opened the door, allowing Satan to exercise power over all that Job had. **2Timothy1:7** *For God has not given us the*

spirit of fear; but of power, and of love, and of a sound mind.
So if God has not given us the spirit of fear, then who did?
Romans 8:15 *For you did not receive the spirit of bondage
again to fear, but you received the Spirit of adoption by whom
we cry out, "Abba, Father."* Fear is bondage and there is actually a spirit of bondage; and where do you think that spirit
comes from? **Hebrews 2:15** *...and deliver them who through
fear of death were all their lifetime subject to bondage.* Job
was in bondage to fear over the spiritual condition of his children; for that reason he was continually offering up sacrifices
to God. Job's attitude and opinion of the nature of God was
not that much different than that of most people today. Many
picture God with a big stick, just waiting for someone to step
out of line; and in some cases ready to whack you anyway
while still standing in line.

After God pointed out to Satan that everything Job had
was in his power, Satan realized that he himself had the
power to steal, kill, and destroy Job's possessions. However,
God also pointed out to Satan that Job's **flesh was not** in his
power. However, that, too, shall change in time.

The first thing Satan does to Job is to kill all of his oxen
and asses and all but one of the attending servants. The first
surviving servant became a "messenger of the evil tidings"
to Job. And while the first messenger was delivering the
evil tidings of Job's loss, a second messenger came and
said, Job 1:16-19 *The fire of God is fallen from heaven and
has burned up all the sheep and servants and I alone have
escaped to bring you these evil tidings. And while he was still
speaking the third messenger came and **said**, three bands
of the Chaldeans stole all your camels and killed all your
servants except me. And while he was still **speaking**, a fourth
messenger came and **said**, your sons and daughters were
eating and drinking wine in their oldest brother's house:
and behold there came a great wind from out of the desert*

knocking down the house and killing all of your children and servants, only I escaped to tell you these evil tidings.

Now if Job wasn't in fear before, he certainly was now! What does the Bible say about listening to evil tidings? **Psalm 112:7** *He shall not be afraid of evil tidings: his heart is fixed, trusting in the LORD.* If those weren't evil tidings, then I am not sure what <u>would</u> qualify. God says, I *have not given you the spirit of fear, but of power, love, and a sound mind.* **2Corinthians 10:5** *...casting down imaginations, and every high thing that exalts itself against the knowledge of God, and bringing into captivity every thought to the obedience of Christ.* Job wasn't casting down imaginations and every high thing that exalts itself against the knowledge of God. No, he was actually giving God the credit for all this evil. **Job 2:10** *...What? Shall we receive good at the hand of God, and **shall we not receive evil?*** **NO! We shall not!** **James 1:13-15** *Let no man say when he is tempted, I am tempted of God: for God cannot be tempted with evil, neither tempts He any man: But every man is tempted, when he is drawn away of his own lust, and enticed. Then when lust hath conceived, it brings forth sin: and sin, when it is finished, brings forth death.*

Job2:10(b) *In all this did not Job sin with his lips.* He did not sin with his lips, but he sure did <u>open the door for Satan</u> to have a "field day" by using what he said against him, as you will see later when Satan returns to God with another accusation and more requests.

Giving God credit for the evil deeds that Satan performs is not in and of itself a sinful act. However, it is an act that will produce negative or devastating results. Voicing ignorant false claims about the nature of God is not a sin, but since our words produce blessings or cursing and create or destroy, our false statements and negative professions give Satan ammunition to launch an attack against us. When you say, "God gives and God takes away" as Job did, you are giving Satan permission to take away or steal from you by the power of the words of your mouth. Job's thoughts and imaginations were fueled by fear and consequently from the abundance of Job's heart his mouth spoke. The words he spoke were not words of faith, but rather words of fear. **Job 3:25** *For the thing which **I greatly feared** is come upon me, and that which **I was afraid of** is come unto me.*

The messenger reported to Job that the fire of God came down from heaven and burned up the sheep. Satan can call down fire from heaven, as it is reported several times in the Bible, and the Antichrist himself in the book of Revelation will do the same. Satan can control the weather and did so with the wind from the desert that resulted in the deaths of Job's children. Satan is referred to as the prince of the power of the air. Even so, all natural disasters are blamed on God and insurance companies actually call these events "acts of God."

One of the first charges that Job levels against God was in **Job 1:21** *Job said, "Naked came I out of my mother's womb, and naked shall I return thither: **the LORD gave, and the LORD hath taken away;** blessed be the name of the LORD."* But Jesus said, *I have come that you might have life and have it more abundantly and the thief is come to steal, kill and destroy.* <u>The Lord gives and Satan takes away!</u> Christians today still quote **Job 1:21**, giving God blame for Satan's work; and then they add, "blessed be the name of the Lord," praising God and blessing him for killing, stealing and destroying. "God called grandma home with cancer because he wanted her more than we did, blessed be the name of the Lord." "Little Billy was run over by a car and the preacher in the gravesite says, God works in mysterious ways... we don't know why this happened only God knows, but he's called Billy home for some reason, it's not for us to know." Oy vey! But remember **Hosea 4:6** *My people are destroyed* *for lack of knowledge: because they have rejected knowledge* (the knowledge of God's word).

Satan comes back to God and God says in **Job 2:3** *Have you considered my servant Job, that there is none like him in the earth, a perfect and an upright man, one that fears God and rejects evil? And still he holds fast his integrity, although you move Me against him* [without success], *to destroy him without cause.* Satan answers, *skin for skin, all that a man has he will give for his life. Put forth your hand now, touch his bone and his flesh, and he will curse you to your face.* He tries to talk God into stretching forth His hand against Job, just like he tried to talk Jesus into turning the stones into bread. **Matthew 4:3** *Now when the tempter came to Him, he said, "If You are the Son of God, command that these stones become bread."* Now does God stretch forth His hand or give Satan permission to attack Job? No! He simply says, *Behold, he is in thine hand, but save his life.* Did God change his mind? Didn't God tell Satan before, do not touch his flesh? Now he says, he is in your hand! What changed? Not God!

Do you think God changes His mind? **Malachi 3:6** declares, *I the LORD do not change. So you, O descendants of Jacob, are not destroyed.* Similarly, **James 1:17** tells us, *Every good and perfect gift is from above, coming down from the Father of the heavenly lights, who does not change like shifting shadows.* The meaning of **Numbers 23:19** could not be clearer: *God is not a man, that He should lie, nor a son of man, that He should change His mind. Does He speak and then not act? Does He promise and not fulfill?* No, God does not change His mind. These verses assert that God is unchanging, and unchangeable.

"I doubt that any Christian would deny the fact that God, being omnipotent (all-powerful), omnipresent (ever-present) and omniscient (all-knowing), could change His mind if He wished, but the question is: Does God **ever** change His mind? Anyone who is all-knowing must, by definition, know everything and therefore should never need to change His mind because He knew what has, and what will, happen in any set of circumstances. His word is quite clear – He knew us before we were born (**Jeremiah 1:5**) so why would He ever need to change His mind?" Graham Pockett

The Bible says in: **Romans 2:11** *For there is no respect of persons with God.* If that is the case, Job is not going to receive special treatment at the whim of God. In that case, whether Job is ignorant of God's laws or not, he is subject to the consequences of breaking God's laws. *My people are destroyed for lack of knowledge: because they have rejected knowledge…* (**the knowledge of God's word**). Job was definitely ignorant when it came to knowledge of whom God is and how he operates. The Scripture says that out of the abundance of the heart the mouth speaks.

Job mouthed 77 false charges against God, as follows:
Job says; God says…

1. *(1:21)* *"God has hedged me in with calamity."* **Psalms 18:18 They confronted me in the day of my calamity, But the LORD was my support.**

2. *(2:10)* *"What? shall we receive good at the hand of God, and shall we not receive evil?."* **James 1:13-14 Let no man say when he is tempted, I am tempted of God: for God cannot be tempted with evil, neither tempt he any man: But every man is tempted, when he is drawn away of his own lust, and enticed. Jesus said, we are to pray…"deliver us from evil"** NOT deliver us from God!

3. *"The Lord gives and the Lord takes away."* **John 10:10 The thief [Satan] cometh not, but for to steal, and to kill, and to destroy: I am come that they might have life, and that they might have it more abundantly.**

4. *"For the Almighty has struck me down with his arrows."* **Psalms 91:5 You shall not be afraid of the terror by night, Nor of the arrow that flies by day,**

5. (6:4) *"He has sent his poisoned arrows deep within my spirit."* **Psalms 91:4 He shall cover you with His feathers, And under His wings you shall take refuge; His truth shall be your shield and buckler.**

6. *"All God's terrors are arrayed against me."* **Psalm 91:4 He shall cover you with His feathers, And under His wings you shall take refuge.**

7. *"You shatter me with dreams."* **8.** *"You terrify me with visions."* **Acts 2:17 And it shall come to pass in the last days, says God, that I will pour out of My Spirit on all flesh; Your sons and your daughters shall prophesy, your young men shall see visions, your old men shall dream dreams.**

9. (7:14) *"I would rather die of strangulation than go on and on like this"*. **Psalms 91:15 He shall call upon Me, and I will answer him; I will be with him in trouble; I will deliver him and honor him.**

10. (7:20)" *Why hast thou set me as a mark against you?"* **Psalms 91:7 A thousand may fall at your side, And ten thousand at your right hand; But it shall not come near you.**

11. (7:21) *"You do not pardon my transgressions."* **Isaiah 44:22 I have blotted out, like a thick cloud, your transgressions, and like a cloud, your sins. Return to Me, for I have redeemed you." Psalms 65:3 Iniquities prevail against me; As for our transgressions, You will provide atonement for them.**

12. (9:17) *"God breaks me with tempest."* **Hebrews 6:19 This hope we have as an anchor of the soul, both sure and steadfast, and which enters the Presence behind the veil.**

13. *"He multiplies my wounds without cause."* **Psalms 147:3 He heals the brokenhearted and binds up their wounds.**

14. (9:18) *"He will not allow me to take my breath."* **Isaiah 42:5 Thus says God the LORD, Who created the heavens and stretched them out, Who spread forth the earth and that which comes from it, Who gives breath to the people on it, And spirit to those who walk on it.**

15." He fills me with bitterness." **Isaiah 61:3 To console those who mourn in Zion, To give them beauty for ashes, The oil of joy for mourning, The garment of praise for the spirit of heaviness; That they may be called trees of righteousness, The planting of the LORD, that He may be glorified."**

16. (9:22) He destroys the perfect with the wicked. **Genesis 18:25 Far be it from You to do such a thing as this, to slay the righteous with the wicked, so that the righteous should be as the wicked; far be it from You! Shall not the Judge of all the earth do right?"**

17. (9:23) "He will laugh at the trial of the innocence."

18. (9:24) "He has given the Earth to the wicked." **Exodus 23:7 Keep yourself far from a false matter; do not kill the innocent and righteous. For I will not justify the wicked.**

19. (10:7-8) "You know that I am not wicked, yet you destroy me." 20. "He hides the faces of the judges so that they cannot discern right and wrong." **Deuteronomy 25:1 If there is a dispute between men, and they come to court, that the judges may judge them, and they justify the righteous and condemn the wicked. Deuteronomy 32:4 He is the Rock, His work is perfect; For all His ways are justice, A God of truth and without injustice; Righteous and upright is He.**

21. (9:30-31) "If I make myself ever so clean, yet you will plunge me into the ditch." **Psalms 40:2 He also brought me up out of a horrible pit, Out of the miry clay, And set my feet upon a rock, And established my steps.**

22. (10:3) "You oppress and despise me." **Psalms 51:17 The sacrifices of God are a broken spirit, A broken and a contrite heart – These, O God, You will not despise.**

23. "You shine upon the Council of the wicked." **Psalms 37:17 For the arms of the wicked shall be broken, But the LORD upholds the righteous.**

24. (10:10) "You have poured me out like milk, and churned me like cheese." **Psalms 91:4-5 Surely He shall** *deliver you from the snare of the fowler And from the perilous pestilence. He shall cover you with His feathers, And under His wings you shall take refuge;*

25. (10:14) "If I sin then you mark me and will not forgive me." Psalms 51:3-10 For I acknowledge my transgressions, And my sin is always before me. Against You, You only, have I sinned, and done this evil in Your sight — that You may be found just when You speak, And blameless when You judge. Behold, I was brought forth in iniquity, and in sin my mother conceived me. Behold, You desire truth in the inward parts, and in the hidden part You will make me to know wisdom. Purge me with hyssop, and I shall be clean; Wash me, and I shall be whiter than snow. Make me hear joy and gladness, that the bones You have broken may rejoice. Hide Your face from my sins, and blot out all my iniquities. Create in me a clean heart, O God, and renew a steadfast spirit within me.

26. (10:16) "You hunt me as a fierce lion." Psalms 91:13 You shall tread upon the lion and the cobra, the young lion and the serpent you shall trample underfoot.

27. (10:17) "You renew your witness against me, and increase wrath upon me." Psalms 91:14-16 14 Because he has set his love upon Me, therefore I will deliver him; I will set him on high, because he has known My name. He shall call upon Me, and I will answer him; I will be with him in trouble; I will deliver him and honor him. With long life I will satisfy him, and show him My salvation."

28. (12:6) "The tabernacles of robbers prosper, and they that provoke God are secure; into whose hand God brings abundance." Psalms 34:16 The face of the LORD [is] against those who do evil, To cut off the remembrance of them from the earth.

29. (13:15) "Though he slay me, yet will I trust him." Proverbs 3:5-6 Trust in the LORD with all your heart, and lean not on your own understanding; In all your ways acknowledge Him, and He shall direct your paths.

30. *(13:24) "You hide your face from me and count me as your enemy." Psalms 27:8 When You said, "Seek My face," My heart said to You, "Your face, LORD, I will seek." 2Chronicles 7:14 If My people who are called by My name will humble themselves, and pray and seek My face, and turn from their wicked ways, then I will hear from heaven, and will forgive their sin and heal their land.*

31. *(13:26) "You write bitter things against me and make me posses the iniquities of my youth." 1John 1:9 If we confess our sins, He is faithful and just to forgive us our sins and to cleanse us from all unrighteousness.*

32. *(13:27) "You put my feet in stocks." Romans 6:18 And having been set free from sin, you became slaves of righteousness. John 8:36 If the Son therefore shall make you free, ye shall be free indeed.*

33. *(14:19) "You destroy the hope of man." Psalms 16:9 Therefore my heart is glad and my glory rejoices: my flesh also shall rest in hope. Psalms 31:24 Be of good courage, and he shall strengthen your heart, all ye that hope in the LORD. Psalms 119:114 Thou art my hiding place and my shield: I hope in your word. Proverbs 13:12 Hope deferred makes the heart sick: but [when] the desire comes, it is a tree of life. 1John 3:3 And every man that hath this hope in him purifies himself, even as he is pure.*

34. *(16:7) "He has made me weary." Galatians 6:9 And let us not be weary in well doing: for in due season we shall reap, if we faint not. 2Thessalonnians 3:13 But ye, brethren, be not weary in well doing. 1Peter 5:7 Cast all your care upon him; for he cares for you.*

35. *"Made desolate all my company." Deuteronomy 28:4 Blessed shall be the fruit of your body, the produce of your ground and the increase of your herds, the increase of your cattle and the offspring of your flocks.*

36. *(16:8)* *"Filled me with wrinkles"* **Deuteronomy 28:11 And the LORD will grant you plenty of goods, *in the fruit of your body*, in the increase of your livestock, and in the produce of your ground, in the land of which the LORD swore to your fathers to give you.**

37. *(16:9)" He tears me in wrath."* **Deuteronomy 28:13 And the LORD will make you the head and not the tail; you shall be above only, and not be beneath...**

38. *"You hate me."* **John 14:21 He who has My commandments and keeps them, it is he who loves Me. And he who loves Me will be loved by My Father, and I will love him and manifest Myself to him.**

39. *"God gnashes upon me with his teeth."* **Romans 8:35 Who shall separate us from the love of Christ? Shall tribulation, or distress, or persecution, or famine, or nakedness, or peril, or sword? Romans 8:39 Nor height nor depth, nor any other created thing, shall be able to separate us from the love of God which is in Christ Jesus our Lord.**

40. *(16:11)* *"He has delivered me to the ungodly, into the hands of the wicked."* **Psalms 18:48 He delivers me from my enemies. You also lift me up above those who rise against me; You have delivered me from the violent man. Psalms 34:4 I sought the LORD, and He heard me, and delivered me from all my fears.**

41. *"He has broken me asunder."* **Psalms 51:17 The sacrifices of God are a broken spirit, a broken and a contrite heart — These, O God, You will not despise.**

42. *"He has taken me by the neck and shaken me to pieces."* **Psalms 61:1-4 HEAR my cry, O God; Attend to my prayer. From the end of the earth I will cry to You, when my heart is overwhelmed; Lead me to the rock that is higher than I. For you have been a shelter for me, A strong tower from the enemy. I will abide in Your tabernacle forever; I will trust in the shelter of Your wings.**

43. *"He has set me out for his mark." Psalms 62:5 My soul, wait silently for God alone, for my expectation is from Him. He only is my rock and my salvation; He is my defense; I shall not be moved. In God is my salvation and my glory; The rock of my strength, and my refuge, is in God. Trust in Him at all times, you people; Pour out your heart before Him; God is a refuge for us.*

44. *(16:13) "His archers compassed me." Deuteronomy 33:29 Happy are you, O Israel! Who is like you, a people saved by the LORD, The shield of your help And the sword of your majesty! Your enemies shall submit to you, and you shall tread down their high places.*

45. *"He cleaves my reins". Psalms 7:9 Oh let the wickedness of the wicked come to an end; but establish the just: for the righteous God tries the hearts and reins. Psalms 26:2 Examine me, O LORD, and prove me; <u>try my reins and my heart</u>. Proverbs 23:16 Yea, <u>my reins shall rejoice</u>, when <u>my lips speak right things.</u>*

46. *"He does not spare me." Romans 8:32 He that spared not his own Son, but delivered him up for us all, how shall he not with him also freely give us all things?*

47. *"He pours out my gall upon the ground." Psalms 1:1-3 Blessed is the man that walks not in the counsel of the ungodly, nor stands in the way of sinners, nor sits in the seat of the scornful. But his delight is in the law of the LORD; and in his law does he meditate day and night. And he shall be like a tree planted by the rivers of water, that brings forth his fruit in his season; his leaf also shall not wither; and what ever he does shall prosper.*

48. *(16:14) "He breaks me with breach upon breach." Isaiah 58:12 Those from among you shall build the old waste places; You shall raise up the foundations of many generations; And you shall be called the Repairer of the Breach, The Restorer of Streets to Dwell In.*

49. *"Runs upon me like a giant." Psalms144:1-2 Blessed be the Lord my Rock, Who trains my hands for war, and my fingers for battle— My loving kindness and my fortress, My high tower and my deliverer, My shield and the One in whom I take refuge, Who subdues my people under me.*

50. *(16:17)" He has done all this for no injustice in my hands." Deuteronomy 32:4 He is the Rock, His work is perfect; for all His ways are justice, a God of truth and without injustice; Righteous and upright is He.*

51. *(17:6) "He has made me a byword of the people." Proverbs 29:2 When the righteous are in authority, the people rejoice; but when a wicked man rules, the people groan.*

52. *(19:6) "God has overthrown me." Proverbs 11:11 By the blessing of the upright the city is exalted, but it is overthrown by the mouth of the wicked. Proverbs 12:7 The wicked are overthrown and are no more, But the house of the righteous will stand. Proverbs 14:11 The house of the wicked will be overthrown, But the tent of the upright will flourish.*

53. *"Incompassed me in His net." Psalms 10:3-9 For the wicked boasts of his heart's desire... His mouth is full of cursing and deceit and oppression;Under his tongue is trouble and iniquity. He sits in the lurking places of the villages; In the secret places he murders the innocent; His eyes are secretly fixed on the helpless. He lies in wait secretly, as a lion in his den; He lies in wait to catch the poor; He catches the poor when he draws him into his net. Psalms 25:15 My eyes are ever toward the LORD, For He shall pluck my feet out of the net. Psalms 31:4 Pull me out of the net which they have secretly laid for me, For You are my strength. Psalms 35:7-8 For without cause they have hidden their net for me in a pit, Which they have dug without cause for my life. Let destruction come upon him unexpectedly, and let his net that he has hidden catch himself; into that very destruction let him fall.*

*54. (19:7)"He does not hear me." **Psalms 86:7 In the day of my trouble I will call upon You, for You will answer me. Psalms 91:15 He shall call upon Me, and I will answer him; I will be with him in trouble; I will deliver him and honor him.***

*55. (19:7) "There is no justice from him." **Deuteronomy 32:4 He is the Rock, His work is perfect; For <u>all His ways are justice</u>, A <u>God of truth and without injustice</u>; Righteous and upright is He.***

*56. (19:8) "He has fenced up my way that I cannot pass." **Galatians 5:1 Stand fast therefore in the liberty wherewith Christ hath made us free, and be not entangled again with the yoke of bondage. Psalms 18:2 The LORD is my rock, and my fortress, and my deliverer; my God, my strength, in whom I will trust; my buckler, and the horn of my salvation, and my high tower.***

*57. "He has set a darkness in my paths." **Proverbs 6:23 For the commandment is a lamp; and the law is light; and reproofs of instruction are the way of life: Psalms 119:105 Your word is a lamp unto my feet, and a light unto my path.***

*58. (19:9) "Stripped me of my glory." **Psalms 29:2 Give unto the LORD the glory due to <u>His name</u>; Worship the LORD in the beauty of holiness. Psalms 62:7 <u>In God</u> is my salvation and my glory; The rock of my strength, and my refuge, is in God.***

*59. "Taken my crown." **James 1:12 Blessed is the man who endures temptation; for when he has been approved, he will receive the crown of life which the Lord has promised to those who love Him. 2Timothy 4:8 Finally, there is laid up for me the crown of righteousness, which the Lord, the righteous Judge, will give to me on that Day, and not to me only but also to all who have loved His appearing. Revelation 2:10 ...Be faithful until death, and I will give you the crown of life. Rev 3:11 Behold, I am coming*** *quickly! Hold fast what you have, that no one may take your crown.*

60. (19:10) "Destroyed me on every side." Psalms 91:5-8 You shall not be afraid of the terror by night, Nor of the arrow that flies by day, Nor of the pestilence that walks in darkness, Nor of the destruction that lays waste at noonday. A thousand may fall at your side, and ten thousand at your right hand; But it shall not come near you. Only with your eyes shall you look, and see the reward of the wicked.

61. "Removed my hope like a tree." Proverbs 13:12 Hope deferred makes the heart sick, But when the desire comes, it is a tree of life. Psalms 31:24 Be of good courage, and He shall strengthen your heart, all you who hope in the LORD. Psalms 119:114 You [are] my hiding place and my shield; I hope in Your word.

62. (19:11) "Kindled his wrath against me." Psalms 2:12 ...when His wrath is kindled but a little. Blessed are all those who put their trust in Him.

63. "Counted me as one of his enemies." James 4:4 ...do you not know that friendship with the world is enmity with God? Whoever therefore wants to be a friend of the world makes himself an enemy of God. John 15:15 Henceforth I call you not servants; for the servant knows not what his lord does: but I have called you friends; for all things that I have heard of my Father I have made known unto you.

64. (19:12) "His troops rise up their way against me, and encamped round my house." Luke 4:10 For it is written, He shall give his angels charge over you, to keep you.

65. "He has put my brethren far from me." Deuteronomy 31:6 Be strong and of good courage, do not fear nor be afraid of them; for the LORD your God, He is the One who goes with you. He will not leave you nor forsake you.

66. (19:13) "Estranged my acquaintances." Psalms 84:11 For the LORD God is a sun and shield; The LORD will give grace and glory; No good thing will He withhold from those who walk uprightly.

67. *(23:16) "The Almighty troubles me." Psalms 27:5 For in the time of trouble he shall hide me in his pavilion: in the secret of his tabernacle shall he hide me; he shall set me up upon a rock. Psalms 37:39 But the salvation of the righteous is of the LORD: he is their strength in the time of trouble.*

68. *(27:2) "God has taken away my judgment."* **Ecclesiastes 2:26** *For God gives wisdom and knowledge and joy to a man who is good in His sight; but to the sinner He gives the work of gathering and collecting, that he may give to him who is good before God. This also is vanity and grasping for the wind.*

69. *"Vexed my soul." Psalms 6:3-9 My soul is also sore vexed: but thou, O LORD, how long? Return, O LORD, deliver my soul: oh save me for your mercies' sake. For in death there is no remembrance of you: in the grave who shall give you thanks? I am weary with my groaning; all the night make I my bed to swim; I water my couch with my tears. My eye is consumed because of grief; it waxes old because of all mine enemies. Depart from me, all ye workers of iniquity; for the LORD hath heard the voice of my weeping. The LORD hath heard my supplication; the LORD will receive my prayer.*

70. *(30:11) "Loosed my cord." Romans 12:2 And do not be conformed to this world, but be transformed by the renewing of your mind, that you may prove what is that good and acceptable and perfect will of God.*

71. *"Afflicted me." John 10:10 The thief does not come except to steal, and to kill, and to destroy. I have come that they may have life, and that they may have it more abundantly.*

72. *(30:19) "Cast me into the mire." Psalms 40:2 He also brought me up out of a horrible pit, Out of the miry clay, And set my feet upon a rock, and established my steps.*

73. "I cried to you and you do not regard me." **Nehemiah 9:27 Therefore You delivered them into the hand of their enemies, Who oppressed them; And in the time of their trouble, When they cried to You, You heard from heaven; And according to Your abundant mercies You gave them deliverers who saved them From the hand of their enemies.**

74. "I stand up and you do not regard me." **Psalms 91:15-16 He shall call upon Me, and I will answer him; I will be with him in trouble; I will deliver him and honor him. With long life I will satisfy him, and show him My salvation.**

75. (30:21) "You have become cruel to me." **Psalms 91:1-4 HE who dwells in the secret place of the Most High shall abide under the shadow of the Almighty. I will say of the LORD, "He is my refuge and my fortress; My God, in Him I will trust." Surely He shall deliver you from the snare of the fowler and from the perilous pestilence. He shall cover you with His feathers, and under His wings you shall take refuge; His truth shall be your shield and buckler.**

76. "You oppose me." **Exodus 23:22 But if you are careful to obey him, following all my instructions, then I will be an enemy to your enemies, and I will oppose those who oppose you.**

77. (30:22) "You have lifted me up to the wind and have dissolved my substance." **Psalms 62:1-2 TRULY my soul silently waits for God; From Him comes my salvation. He only is my rock and my salvation. He is my defense; I shall not be greatly moved.**

Is it any wonder these words of Job opened the door for Satan to "...kill, steal, and destroy..."? If Job were to present these charges in a court of law, he would lose hands down, for not one of these charges would hold up.

Fear was the root cause or motivating influence behind Job's misguided accusations and unfounded claims directed at God. Just as the foundation for faith is knowledge, fear stems from the lack of knowledge in an unsound mind. *For God has not given us the spirit of fear, but of love, power and a sound mind.*

CHAPTER 5

Fear: A Disease Of The Soul

The Book of Job is an instruction manual on how to avoid unnecessary suffering as a result of courting the spirit of fear. Fear is the common denominator for many of man's mental and physical diseases, ranging from phobias to asthma, high blood pressure, strokes and nervous conditions. Fear-filled words have power to curse, destroy, tear down, discourage, depress, malign, and even call into being death and disease.

A dangerous misconception of fear is that it is a natural necessary emotion. Many people allow fear to control their lives and accept fear as a normal way of life. If fear were natural, then it would be listed as one of God's gifts to man; however, God's word warns of the destructiveness of the spirit of fear and announces that, *God has not given us the spirit of fear, but of love, power and a strong mind.* (**2Timothy 1:6-7**) A sound mind is a mind that is "free from fear." A mind tormented with fearful thoughts is anything but sound. Fear enters our mind as a seed (thought), it sprouts, takes root and begins to grow. When we act on this thought or speak it out, acknowledging it, the fear now becomes a stronghold. The Bible warns us to cast down every thought that exalts itself above the knowledge and truth of God's Word. **2Corinthians**

10:5 *Casting down imaginations, and every high thing that exalts itself against the knowledge of God, and bringing into captivity every thought to the obedience of Christ.* Fear itself has no power; the power comes from our spoken words that are motivated by the spirit of fear. Satan can use these words against us to bring to pass the negative words that we speak, just as God uses our faith-filled words to manifest His power through us.

The number one goal for Satan is to destroy our faith in God. His second goal is to destroy our faith in as many of God's promises as he can. God says, "I will provide all of your needs according to my riches in glory by Christ Jesus." Satan will get you to confess lack and give you the spirit of poverty and depression. He wants to rob you of your joy and peace and replace it with fear, worry, stress, concern, care, anxiety, lack, depression and hopelessness. Jesus took your sickness, disease and infirmities on the cross. Like salvation, healing is a gift that cannot be earned, only freely received by faith. Satan wants you to believe that God allows him to put sickness on you to teach you some kind of a lesson so you won't ask him for healing, because if you do, you will be praying against God's will for you.

Fear is the foundation of unbelief and Satan's most powerful weapon of choice. Satan counterfeits all of God's blessings, promises and holy attributes. What is the greatest thing you could do for God? Love Him? Serve Him? Seek Him? Honor Him? **Ecclesiastes 12:13** *Let us hear the conclusion of the whole matter: Fear God, and keep his commandments: for this is the whole duty of man.* **Proverbs 19:23** *The fear of the LORD tends to life: and he that has it shall abide satisfied; he shall not be visited with evil.* **Proverbs 15:33** *The fear of the LORD is the instruction of wisdom; and before honor is humility.* The fear of God is a righteous, holy fear, a wise fear. A fear of God brings wisdom! **Proverbs**

9:10 *The fear of the LORD is the beginning of wisdom: and the knowledge of the holy is understanding.*

Do you now see why Satan's weapon of choice is fear? Because our source of the greatest power is from fearing God. However Satan's fear is perverted fear: fear that terrorizes, paralyzes, horrifies, destroys our hope, steals our joy, and brings pain, suffering, sickness, disease, calamity, devastation and death. Holy, righteous, Godly fear, results in *wisdom and understanding;* for *The fear of the Lord is the beginning of wisdom:and the knowledge is understanding.*

There are hundreds of phobias or spirits of fear that literally control peoples lives, keeping them in bondage. **Romans 8:15** *For ye have not received the spirit of bondage again to fear; but ye have received the Spirit of adoption, whereby we cry, Abba, Father.* **Hosea 4:6** says, *My people are destroyed for lack of knowledge: because thou hast rejected knowledge, I will also reject thee.* **2Timothy 1:7** *For God has not given us a spirit of fear, but of power and of love and of a sound mind.* So, if God says, *He has not given you the spirit of fear,* then where did it come from? Fear is the exact opposite of faith; fear is to faith what darkness is to light. God said "let there be light" and His Word created light, His Word is light, Jesus is light! Jesus said in **John 8:12** *Then spake Jesus again unto them, saying, I am the light of the world: he that follows me shall not walk in darkness, but shall have the light of life.* **John 12:46** *I am come a light into the world, that whosoever believeth on me should not abide in darkness.* Until God spoke His Word, *Let there be light…the earth was without form, and void; and darkness was upon the face of the deep. And the Spirit of God moved upon the face of the waters. And God saw the light, that it was good: and God divided the light from the darkness.* **Genesis 1:2-4**

God's Word *separates the light from the darkness;* God's Word is light, Satan's word is darkness (void of light). **2Samuel 22:29** *For you are my lamp, O LORD: and the*

LORD will lighten my darkness. We all have experienced Achluophobia (fear of darkness) at some time in our life. Why is this one so common or universal? Darkness is the absence of light! How profound. Actually it is not so much the darkness that we are afraid of as it is not being able to see. The darkness renders us blind, unable to see what the darkness is concealing. Then the spirit of fear enters our mind, controlling our thoughts until we are consumed by the reality of darkness. Our thoughts begin controlling our imaginations which, in turn, fuel the "fear factor." This vicious cycle continues unchecked until we are paralyzed by fear and surrender to panic and hopelessness. Is it any wonder that Satan's favorite weapon of choice is fear? **1Peter 5:8** warns us to *be sober, be vigilant; because your adversary the devil, as a roaring lion, walks about, seeking whom he may devour...Satan has come to kill, steal and destroy.* The root of Job's misery was fear: **Job 3:25** *For the thing I greatly feared has come upon me, and what I feared has happened to me.* With the use of fear Satan will get you to confess poverty or lack, sickness, disease or infirmities, sadness, depression, hopelessness, suicide, or defeat; the results are anxiety, stress, high blood pressure, stroke, heart attack, mental illness, or death! Jesus said, *I have come that you might have life and have it more abundantly and the thief* [Satan] *has come to kill, steal and destroy.*

To give you some perspective of Satan's stranglehold on man through fear, I have listed the phobias beginning with the letter "A". If you respond as I did, you will find most of these ridiculous and may even think they are made up. Sadly, each of them are someone's "real" fears and Satan has them in bondage. To add insult to injury, these same tormented people live in silent fear to avoid ridicule, embarrassment and humiliation from others who judge the validity and authenticity of their fear.

Ablutophobia- Fear of washing or bathing.
Acarophobia- Fear of itching or of the insects that cause itching.
Acerophobia- Fear of sourness.
Achluophobia- Fear of darkness.
Acousticophobia- Fear of noise.
Acrophobia- Fear of heights.
Aerophobia- Fear of drafts, air swallowing, or airborne noxious substances.
Aeroacrophobia- Fear of open high places.
Aeronausiphobia- Fear of vomiting secondary to airsickness.
Agateophobia- Fear of insanity.
Agliophobia- Fear of pain.
Agoraphobia- Fear of open spaces or of being in crowded, public places like markets;
Fear of leaving a safe place.
Agraphobia- Fear of sexual abuse.
Agrizoophobia- Fear of wild animals.
Agyrophobia- Fear of streets or crossing the street.
Aichmophobia- Fear of needles or pointed objects.
Ailurophobia- Fear of cats.
Albuminurophobia- Fear of kidney disease.
Alektorophobia- Fear of chickens.
Algophobia- Fear of pain.
Alliumphobia- Fear of garlic.
Allodoxaphobia- Fear of opinions.
Altophobia- Fear of heights.
Amathophobia- Fear of dust.
Amaxophobia- Fear of riding in a car.
Ambulophobia- Fear of walking.
Amnesiphobia- Fear of amnesia.
Amychophobia- Fear of scratches or being scratched.
Anablephobia- Fear of looking up.
Ancraophobia- Fear of wind. (Anemophobia)

Androphobia- Fear of men.

Anemophobia- Fear of air drafts or wind.(Ancraophobia)

Anginophobia- Fear of angina, choking or narrowness.

Anglophobia- Fear of England or English culture, etc.

Angrophobia - Fear of anger or of becoming angry.

Ankylophobia- Fear of immobility of a joint.

Anthrophobia or Anthophobia- Fear of flowers.

Anthropophobia- Fear of people or society.

Antlophobia- Fear of floods.

Anuptaphobia- Fear of staying single.

Apeirophobia- Fear of infinity.

Aphenphosmphobia- Fear of being touched. (Haphephobia)

Apiphobia- Fear of bees.

Apotemnophobia- Fear of persons with amputations.

Arachibutyrophobia- Fear of peanut butter sticking to the
    roof of the mouth.

Arachnephobia or Arachnophobia- Fear of spiders.

Arithmophobia- Fear of numbers.

Arrhenphobia- Fear of men.

Arsonphobia- Fear of fire.

Asthenophobia- Fear of fainting or weakness.

Astraphobia or Astrapophobia- Fear of thunder and
    lightning (Ceraunophobia, Keraunophobia).

Astrophobia- Fear of stars or celestial space.

Asymmetriphobia- Fear of asymmetrical things.

Ataxiophobia- Fear of ataxia. (muscular incoordination)

Ataxophobia- Fear of disorder or untidiness.

Atelophobia- Fear of imperfection.

Atephobia- Fear of ruin or ruins.

Athazagoraphobia- Fear of being forgotten or ignored or
    forgetting.

Atomosophobia- Fear of atomic explosions.

Atychiphobia- Fear of failure.

Aulophobia- Fear of flutes.

Aurophobia- Fear of gold.

Auroraphobia- Fear of Northern lights.

Autodysomophobia- Fear of one that has a vile odor.

Automatonophobia- Fear of ventriloquist's dummies, animatronic creatures, or wax statues – anything that falsely represents a sentient being.

Automysophobia- Fear of being dirty.

Autophobia- Fear of being alone or of oneself.

Aviophobia or Aviatophobia- Fear of flying.

For the complete list you can log on to: http://www.phobialist.com

My favorite was: Hippopotomonstrosesquippedaliophobia- Fear of long words.

If you resist fear, Satan has no access into your life. When you refuse fear, you paralyze Satan; and he can't harm you. *The fear of the LORD tends to life: and he that has it shall abide satisfied; **he shall not be visited with evil.*** **2Timothy 1:7** *For God has not given us a spirit of fear, but of power and of love and of a sound mind.* **1John 4:18** *There is **no fear in love; but perfect love casts out fear**: because fear has torment. He that fears is not made perfect in love.*

You can't believe God's Word and be fearful at the same time. For you to say "I am afraid" is for you to enter into unbelief and deny God's Word. For a believer not to believe God's Word and to fear is opening the door for Satan's attack. Anything that doesn't line up with the Word of God is an invitation to the enemy. For a believer not to believe God's Word and to fear is wicked and has potentially serious consequences. **Revelation 21:8** *But the **fearful, and unbelieving**, and the abominable, and murderers, and whoremongers, and sorcerers, and idolaters, and all liars, shall have their part in the lake which burns with fire and brimstone: which is the second death.* **Hebrews 11:6** *But **without faith it is impossible to please God**: for he that comes to God **must believe** *that he is who He says He is, and that he rewards those that diligently seek him.*

Fear denies God access into your life. He can't move on your behalf if you won't believe Him. *The thing you fear the most will come upon you.* (**Job 3:25**) Fear will connect you to whatever it is you fear, just as faith will connect you to God's promises. The fear of loss and what is familiar will connect you to poverty; conversely, belief in God's promise in the Bible that if you *seek first the kingdom of God and His righteousness, all these things shall be added unto you.* **Matthew 6:33** Fear will connect you to sickness and disease and faith in God's Word will connect you to the promise that *no plague shall come near your dwelling.* Jesus said I *have taken your disease and sickness on the cross. Thy will be done on earth as it is in heaven.*

Job submitted to fear and lost his family, property, possessions and health!

You are not subject to the world's belief system which is orchestrated by Satan. The world wants you to believe that the flu is out there waiting for you and you should get your flu shot. The world says that you may already have this disease, or statistics show you will more than likely get it so you should "ask your doctor if this drug is right for you." One out of four commercials is promoting drugs or health-related products. **Psalms 112:7** *He shall not be afraid of evil tidings: his heart is fixed, trusting in the LORD.* **Hebrews 2:14-15** *Forasmuch then as the children are partakers of flesh and blood, he also himself likewise took part of the same; that through death Jesus might destroy him that had the power of death, that is, the devil; And deliver them who through fear of death were all their lifetime subject to bondage.* Sickness and death is a curse and Jesus took our sickness on the cross and died for us, becoming the curse for us that through Him we might have healing and eternal life.

Galatians 3:13 *Christ has redeemed us from the curse of the law, having become a curse for us.*

There is no need to fear death, because you hold the power of life and death in your tongue. **Proverbs 18:21** *Death and life are in the power of the tongue, and those who love it will eat its fruit.* You are the establishing witness; you can either produce life or death with the words of your mouth. Your words will determine your destiny for you have a free will to choose life or death: Things don't work for Christians who break the laws or don't understand them. **Deuteronomy 30:19** *I call heaven and earth as witnesses today against you that I have set before you life and death, blessing and cursing; therefore choose life, that both you and your descendants may live.*

What you are afraid of is directly related to your lack of faith in God's Word or what you don't believe to be true. Discover the promises in the Word of God and put your trust and faith in Jesus Christ; then fear will flee, along with doubt and unbelief, and the promises will become a reality in your life. Fear is designed to create doubt and doubt destroys faith and trust. A barometer of your faith is the words of your mouth. They will reveal what is in your heart, for: *A good man out of the good treasure of his heart brings forth good; and an evil man out of the evil treasure of his heart brings forth evil. For out of the abundance of the heart his mouth speaks.* **Luke 6:45**

Examine your life and determine if the negative circumstances are in direct proportion to your words and the confessions of your mouth. Are you experiencing financial problems or some other lack in your life or relationships? Are you confirming these situations and predicaments verbally and announcing from your mouth to others how bad things seem to be? You're not alone! Job and millions of others have done the same thing and got the same results. The thing that you are afraid will happen, **will** happen, and the thing you are afraid will come upon you, **will** come upon you. That's how fear and fear-filled words work! So repent for your unbelief and move on.

Psalms 119:11 *Your word I have hidden in my heart, that I might not sin against You.*

Proverbs 2:1-5 My *son, if you will receive my words, and hide my commandments in your heart; So that you incline your ear to wisdom, and apply your heart to understanding; Yes, if you cry after knowledge, and lift up your voice for understanding; If you seek her as silver, and search for her as for hidden treasures; Then you shall understand the fear of the LORD, and find the knowledge of God.*

CHAPTER 6

The Righteousness of Self

L adies and gentlemen of the jury, here is my closing statement. The court has established, through the introduction of a list of 77 claims and accusations filed by the claimant Mr. Job, that he has allegedly suffered astronomical financial loss, severe personal injury and massive, undue psychological trauma and stress as a result of my Client, God, and His alleged involvement in a wager between Him and Mr. Satan. My rebuttal and summation clearly and undeniably have addressed each charge, claim and accusation; and I have proven beyond a shadow of a doubt that every one of them is false and unfounded. I argue that the character and reputation of my Client, God, has not only been besmirched by these unfounded accusations, claims and charges, but in addition there is now a best selling book that has published these false charges. Now millions of ignorant, unsuspecting readers are accepting Mr. Job's claims about my Client in Job's book as the Gospel, rather than doing research on their own to establish the truth. I would highly recommend that they do their own research. I rest my case!

The charges themselves reveal a clear picture of the nature of God as seen through Job's eyes. What amazes me is the fact that, despite the horrendous loss and pain, both physiological and physiological, Job did not curse God — especially since He thought God Himself was the perpetrator. Even after his wife suggested that he do so: **Job 2:9** *Do you still hold fast to your integrity? Curse God and die!* He responds with, *you speak as one of the foolish women speaks. Shall we indeed accept good from God, and shall we not accept adversity?*

The account of Job reveals that...*he was perfect and upright, and one that feared God, and shunned evil...and his sons went and feasted in their houses every one his day; and sent and called for their three sisters, to eat and to drink with them. And it was so, when the days of their feasting were gone about, that Job sent and sanctified them, and rose up early in the morning, and offered burnt offerings according to the number of them all: for Job said, It may be that my sons have sinned, and cursed God in their hearts. Thus did Job continually.*

Job was not your typical, average man of God. He was perfect, upright, God-fearing, and shunned evil. According to Satan's verbal observation, **Job 1:10** Have *you not made a hedge about him, and about his house, and about all that he has on every side? You have blessed the work of his hands, and his substance is increased in the land.* He was blessed beyond his own expectations — children and wealth in abundance, honor and notoriety. An appropriate scripture might be, *good measure, pressed down, shaken together, and running over.* **Luke 6:38.**

But Job needed to be tested. By God? No! **James 1:13-14** Let *no man say when he is tempted/tested, I am tempted/tested of God: for God cannot be tempted/tested with evil, neither does He tempt/test, any man.* But every man is tempted, when he is drawn away of his own lust, and enticed. I believe there was a deep moral root of self-righteousness in his heart which needed to be laid bare and which had to be brought to the surface and acknowledged. Indeed, we may discern this lack of self examination in his very own words. He says, *It may be that my sons have sinned.* He can't fathom the possibility of sinning himself. Contrast this with what David said in **Psalms 51:** *According to Your loving kindness; according to the multitude of Your tender mercies, Blot out my transgressions. Wash me thoroughly from my iniquity, and cleanse me from my sin. For I acknowledge my transgressions, and my sin is always before me. Against You, You only, have I sinned, nd done this evil in Your sight — that You may be found just when You speak, And blameless when You judge. O Lord, open my lips, And my mouth shall show forth Your praise. For You do not desire sacrifice, or else I would give it; You do not delight in burnt offering. The sacrifices of God are a broken spirit, a broken and a contrite heart—these, O God, You will not despise.*

Even though Job did not sin with his lips (**Job 2:10** *In all this Job did not sin with his lips*) he was harboring self-righteousness in his heart and profusely defended his innocence to his three friends. It was Job's false charges and accusations hurled at God that opened the door for Satan's attacks, and provided the catalyst for Job's contrition and repentance. Job was unaware that this chain of events was initiated by the words of his own mouth (tongue), not by God.

I assert that Job's Lament in Chapter 29 reveals the self-righteous condition of his heart. You get the sense that he was either unaware of it or that he realized *that in me, that is, in my flesh, dwells no good thing.* **Romans 7:18.**

Job 29: *Oh, that I were as in months past, as in the days when God watched over me; when His lamp shone upon my head, aAnd when by His light I walked through darkness; just as I was in the days of my prime, when the friendly counsel of God was over my tent; when the Almighty was yet with me, when my children were around me; when my steps were bathed with cream, and the rock poured out rivers of oil for me! When I went out to the gate by the city, when I* *took my seat in the open square, the young men saw me and hid, and the aged arose and stood; The princes refrained from talking, and put their hand on their mouth; The voice of nobles was hushed, and their tongue stuck to the roof of their mouth. When the ear heard, then it blessed me, and when the eye saw, then it approved me; Because I delivered the poor who cried out, the fatherless and the one who had no helper. The blessing of a perishing man came upon me, and I caused the widow's heart to sing for joy. I put on righteousness, and it clothed me; my justice was like a robe and a turban. I was eyes to the blind, and I was feet to the lame. I was a father to the poor, and I searched out the case that I did not know. I broke the fangs of the wicked, and plucked the victim from his teeth. Then I said, I shall die in my nest, and multiply my days as the sand. My root is spread out to the waters, and the dew lies all night on my branch. My glory is fresh within me, and my bow is renewed in my hand. Men listened to me and waited, and kept silence for my counsel. After my words they did not speak again, and my speech settled on them as dew. They waited for me as for the rain, and they opened their mouth wide as for the spring rain. If I mocked at them, they did not believe it, and the light of my countenance they did not cast down. I chose the way for them, and sat as chief, so I dwelt as a king in the army, as one who comforts mourners. But now they that are younger than I have me in derision, whose fathers I would have disdained to have set with the dogs of my flock.*

This, truly, is a classic sob story. We listen in vain for the slightest hint of a broken and a contrite spirit. There is no indication of self-loathing or disgust. We cannot find so much as a single expression of guilt, vulnerability or human weakness. As you read this chapter, were you cognizant of the number of times he used "me," "my" and "I"? He used them **51** times and referred to God only **5** times. In **Psalms 51** David mentions God **32** times and "I," "my" and "me"

35 times in reference to him being a sinner, transgressor, shaped in iniquity, conceived in sin, desiring cleansing, washing, purging, forgiveness, wisdom, joy and gladness, a clean heart and renew a right spirit, restore his salvation, teach transgressors and convert sinners, sing aloud of God's righteousness, mouth show forth praise, ask for a broken spirit, contrite heart. In contrast, in **Job 29** the "I," "my" and "me" is influential, prestigious, important, exalted, honored, praised, recognized, envied, a hero, judge, revered, King, savior of the poor, fatherless and widows, and more.

In Job's unwavering verbal expression of the unfairness and injustice of God, he revealed the self-righteous condition of his heart. This self-righteous attitude was the breeding ground that produced the negative words spoken from the depths of Job's heart. Oh, woe is me, this is so unfair, I don't deserve this, but God is still great! ...and even if He kills me, I will still worship Him. Oy vey!

Job was humbled through his ordeal, by whom, God? No, but through the trials and tribulation brought on by his own doing. *Behold Satan, everything he has is in your power.* Why? Because of Job's tongue! The words of his mouth—he was the architect of his own undoing.

Chapter 30 is a glowing contrast to chapter 29. It seems Job benefited from Satan's trials in that he saw how superficial and shallow the world is. Those that flattered him in his prosperity shun him now and show contempt. This lesson only brought bitterness: *But now they that are younger than I have me in derision, whose fathers I would have disdained to have set with the dogs of my flock.*

Out of the abundance of the heart Job continues to speak: *They were children of fools, yea, children of base men; they were viler than the earth. And now am I their song, yea, I am their by-word. They abhor me, they flee far from me, and spare not to spit in my face. Because He hath loosed my cord, and afflicted me, they have also let loose the bridle before me. Upon my right hand rise the youth; they push away my feet, and they raise up against me the ways of their destruction. They mar my path, they set forward my calamity, they have no helper. They came upon me as a wide breaking in of waters: in the desolation they rolled themselves upon me.*

Lamenting over the power and possessions Job used to have and maligning his fellow men are not the characteristics of a righteous man with a pure heart. At what point in this story did Job cease from *not sinning with his lips* (**Job 2:10**) and begin needing to repent to God: *therefore I abhor myself, and repent in dust and ashes* (**Job 42:6**)?

What man living now or at any time can compare himself to Job and his ability to endure pain and suffering to the capacity he did, without shaking his fist at God? Before answering, consider the fact that Job had neither the Bible (Old or New Testament) nor the power of the Holy Spirit to see him through. Yet, in the light of our Savior Jesus Christ there is no comparison! Job completely caves under his heavy trials. He not only spews forth a caldron of bitter criticism upon those who opposed him, but then proceeds to curse the day of his birth. **Job 3:1-3** *After this opened Job his mouth and cursed his day. And Job spoke and said, let the day perish wherein I was born, and the night in which it was said, there is a manchild conceived.* As a matter of fact, Job's performance did not bring glory to God's name; however, his contrite heart and repentance did. He humbled himself before God in **Job 40:4**: *Behold, I am vile; what shall I answer You? I lay my hand over my mouth. Once I have spoken, but I will not answer; Yes, twice, but I will proceed no further.* And again in **Job 42:5-6:** *I have heard of You by the hearing of the ear, but now my eye sees You. Therefore I abhor myself, and repent in dust and ashes.*

There are many Bible scholars who believe that the premise of Job was for God to teach Job a lesson. *And the Lord said unto Satan, Have you considered my servant Job, that there is none like him in the earth, a perfect and an upright man, one that fears God and shuns evil? And still he holds fast his integrity.* Satan suggested to God that He stretch forth His hand and destroy the family of this **perfect and upright man who fears God and shuns evil,** and destroy everything he owns and give him a hideous disease from head to foot. Then does God says to go ahead, give it your best shot? How could anyone possibly believe that and still call himself a Bible scholar? Pardon me, I digress!

How much more grievous trials would be without good friends to bless and comfort you! Or would they? Let's see what Job has to say about it: **Job 2:11-13** *Now when Job's three friends heard of all this adversity that had come upon him, each one came from his own place—Eliphaz the Temanite, Bildad the Shuhite, and Zophar the Naamathite. For they had made an appointment together to come and mourn with him, and to comfort him. And when they raised their eyes from afar, and did not recognize him, they lifted their voices and wept; and each one tore his robe and sprinkled dust on his head toward heaven. So they sat down with him on the ground seven days and seven nights, and no one spoke a word to him, for they saw that his grief was very great.*

Eliphaz was the first friend. *Then Eliphaz the Temanite answered and said, If we essay to commune with you, will you be grieved? But who can withhold himself from speaking? Behold, you have instructed many, and you have strengthened the weak hands. Your words have upheld him that was falling, and you have strengthened the feeble knees. But now it is come upon you, and you faint; it touches you, and you are troubled. Is not this your fear, your confidence, your hope, and the uprightness of your ways? Remember, I pray you, whoever perished, being innocent? Or where were the righteous cut off? Even as I have seen, they that plow iniquity, and sow wickedness, reap the same* **(Job 4:1-8)**. *And* *again, I have seen the foolish taking root; but suddenly I cursed his habitation* (**Job 5:3**; see also **Job 15:17**).

Eliphaz was trying to comfort Job by arguing from a position of his own personal **experience**, hence the phrase, *as I have seen.* Now, that would be just fine if the person you were trying to convince was laboring under the same circumstances. Otherwise, what basis do you have to present or argue your point? Case in point, how could Eliphaz possibly relate his life experience with Job's? No two cases are exactly similar, so why even bother to interject yours into the mix? That was exactly the sentiment of Job, for no sooner had Eliphaz finished speaking than, without the slightest recognition or response to his words, Job proceeded with his own tale of woes, interspersed with self-vindication and bitter complaints against God (**Job 6:7**).

Bildad is the second well-meaning friend. He proceeds with an entirely different approach than Eliphaz. He does not refer to personal experience, or even to what he himself has observed. He appeals to others' past experiences. *For inquire, please, of the former age, and consider the things discovered by their fathers, for we were born yesterday, and know nothing, because our days on earth are a shadow. Will they not teach you and tell you and utter words from their heart?* (**Job 8:8-10**) Well, if the twisted theology and parched paradigms of Mathew Henry are any indication of wisdom or revelation knowledge derived from the traditions and counsel from our forefathers, then I can understand why we are exhorted to *study to show yourself approved unto God, a workman that needs not to be ashamed, rightly dividing the word of truth.* (**2Timothy 2:15**) Get your revelations and truths from God's word by the Holy Spirit, not solely from man. If you receive the word from a man, *do not believe every spirit, but test the spirits, whether they are of God; because many false prophets have gone out into the world.* (**1John 4:1**)

Bildad offers a much wider range of possibilities, both for finding answers and formulating questions. He offers the adage that there is safety in numbers as to obtaining reasonably truthful answers to life's difficult questions. Hence, there is more assurance, authority, experience and respectability through many "fathers" than through the limited experience of one individual. It would also hint at **Proverbs 11:14** *Where there is no counsel, the people fall; But in the multitude of counselors there is safety.* In the letter of historical facts experience may ring true; however, in the spirit of historical experience, you cannot find two men whose lives will parallel each other as to causal experiences. As for the traditions of men, their origins and foundations are shaky or nebulous at best. Neither experience nor tradition will judge on That Day, but only God's Word!

Therefore, as might be expected, Bildad's oration carried no more weight with Job than that of Eliphaz. Both efforts were empty and vain, carrying little to no comfort or solace. As far as their assessment of Job's relationship to God, they were 180 degrees off. They concluded Job must have sinned, Job insisted he didn't, and God backed him up. His friends were quick to judge Job based upon their own self-righteous view of the circumstances, from their own perspective, not God's. God's Word is the only standard and His is the only authority qualified to judge. By that standard alone, all men will be judged, and to Him every knee shall bow and every tongue shall confess that Jesus Christ is Lord!

If Job's friends had wielded words of compassion, comfort and encouragement rather than judgment and condemnation, they could have softened the unrelenting blows of the enemy. What's more, compassion and soft, tender words could expose Job's negative, distorted verbal assessment of God and perhaps even revealed the true root cause and source of his afflictions, the words of his mouth and the corresponding attacks of Satan.

Now comes Job's third friend, Zophar: *But oh, that God would speak, and open His lips against you, that He would show you the secrets of wisdom! For they would double your prudence. Know therefore that God exacts from you less than your iniquity deserves. If you would prepare your heart, and stretch out your hands toward Him; if iniquity were in your hand, and you put it far away, and would not let wickedness dwell in your tents; then surely you could lift up your face without spot; Yes, you could be steadfast, and not fear.* **(Job 11:5-6; 13-15)**

Job probably thought something like: how could this so-called friendly motivational seminar get any more depressing; and then comes Zophar. This guy's character assassination of God made Job's assertions seem less severe. To put it mildly, he did not know the Divine Character of God. How could anyone that claims to know God suggest that He could *open His lips against... his servant Job, a man that God himself says that there is none like him on the earth, a blameless and upright man, one who fears God and shuns evil, And still he holds fast to his integrity* — who has just had his entire family destroyed, everything he owns stolen or destroyed, and has been stricken with a dreadful disease?

How is Zophar any different from over 95% of the so-called theologians throughout the decades teaching these same fallacies and recording them in books? God is not against us... **Romans 8:31** *What then shall we say to these things? If God is for us, who can be against us?* He is not a legal exactor, as accused by Zophar (*Know therefore that God exacts from you...*) He is a liberal giver! *I have come that you might have life and have it more abundantly.* **John 10:10** Then again, Zophar says, *If you prepare your heart.* It is obvious he does not have a clue how to do that! If no man is good and all our hearts are desperately wicked, then how is that accomplished? As if he knew. What if he sets out to prepare his heart and finds nothing but evil and finds himself perfectly powerless? Then what? Zophar hasn't got a clue. He only knows God as a heartless exactor who can only *open His lips against you.*

Are you surprised that Zophar had no better success in converting Job to his way of thinking than either of the other two so-called "good" friends? They all were horribly torqued in their opinions; much like today there are spiritual leaders who are trying to figure out God by using legalisms, experience, and the traditions of men. (*And He said unto them, Full well ye reject the commandment of God, that ye may keep your own tradition,* **Mark 7:9.**)

What did Job's friends accomplish in their feeble attempts to counsel or comfort him? *Professing themselves to be wise, they became fools, and changed the glory of the incorruptible God into an image made like to corruptible man.* (**Romans 1:22**) *Who is this who darkens counsel by words without knowledge?* (**Job 38:2**) They are doing to Job what Job did to God. *Job speaks without knowledge, his words are without wisdom.* (**Job 34:35**)

It is evident, by listening to the exhortations of Job's three friends, that they did not have a personal relationship with him. This was evidenced by the lack of compassion, empathy, or intimate understanding of Job's predicament, and especially their lack of trust in Job's assessment of his relationship with his God. I believe that this encounter between Job and his friends is analogous to the relationship of many pastors to their congregations as well as the relationship of most Christians to God. The key word is "personal." A personal, intimate, loving and trusting relationship is born out of faith in someone, which stems from knowing everything about them, their nature, character, values and core beliefs. Hence, to develop a close personal relationship with God requires faith in Him. How can anyone have faith in someone they do not know? (**Romans 10:17**) So then, faith comes by hearing, and hearing by the word of God. The Word of God teaches us what God is like, His nature, character and His righteousness. Faith comes by hearing His Word, and the more of His Word we hear, the more we will know about Him and the more faith we will have in Him. If Job's friends could have looked at Job the way God looked at Job, and the way God saw Job, they would have approached him with love and compassion, looking for a way to *bring him up out of a horrible pit, out of the miry clay, and set his feet upon a rock, and established his steps* (**Psalms 40:2**), and lead him into the light, not into darkness and despair.

The ministry of Job's three friends fell far short of silencing his relentless self-righteous rant at God's supposed injustice, but rather drove him into deeper despair and fueled his feeble attempt at vindication. He now digs in his heels and furiously lashes back in his defense of "self." Then Job spoke again: **Job 12** *You really know everything, don't you? And when you die, wisdom will die with you! Well, I know a few things myself—and you're no better than I am. Who doesn't know these things you've been saying? Look, I have seen many instances such as you describe. I understand what you are saying. I know as much as you do. You are no better than I am. Oh, how I long to speak directly to the Almighty. I want to argue my case with God himself. For you are smearing me with lies. As doctors, you are worthless quacks. Please be quiet! That's the smartest thing you could do. Listen to my charge; pay attention to my arguments. Are you defending God by means of lies and dishonest arguments? You should be impartial witnesses, but will you slant your testimony in his favor? Will you argue God's case for Him? Be careful that He doesn't find out what you are doing! Or do you think you can fool Him as easily as you fool people? No, you will be in serious trouble with Him if even in your hearts you slant your testimony in His favor.*

Doesn't His majesty strike terror into your heart? Does not your fear of Him seize you? Your statements have about as much value as ashes. Your defense is as fragile as a clay pot. Be silent now and leave me alone. Let me speak, and I will face the consequences. Yes, I will take my life in my hands and say what I really think. God might kill me, but I cannot wait. I am going to argue my case with Him. But this is what will save me: that I am not godless. If I were, I would be thrown from His presence. (**Job 13**)

Out of the abundance of the heart the mouth speaks. It is obvious that Job was still far from having a broken spirit or contrite heart. Sure, his friends were wrong in their assessment of Job's heart, the heart of God and in the way they dealt with Job. However, their deplorable behavior does not make Job right! If Job had been quick to condemn and humble himself and acknowledge that he had a self-righteous, self-aggrandizing attitude, he would have stopped his friends' mouths and they would have had nothing to say. And, in turn, if they had spoken with compassion, tenderness and truly offered support, he would have melted instead of hardening his heart. Job insisted he had done nothing wrong and they insinuated he had done nothing right, leaving no room for agreement or understanding. They were headed down two separate roads that never intersected.

CHAPTER 7

Judge Yourself Or Be Judged

The wisest, most appropriate and possibly God-inspired words to be spoken by Job are found in **Job 13:23:** *How many are my iniquities and sins? Make me know my transgression and my sin.* Would you agree that this utterance from Job just might possibly qualify as an unintended prayer, with a slight hint of an indirect cry to God for help? This is one of the last things Job utters prior to God sending a messenger to enlighten him. **Job 31:35** *Let the Almighty show me that I am wrong.*

Job's three friends refused to reply further to him because he kept insisting on his innocence. Here Elihu, with such ease and clarity, seizes upon the very root cause of this major conflict. He distills the convoluted matter contained in 29 chapters into two brief sentences. Job justified himself instead of justifying God, and they had condemned Job instead of leading him to condemn himself. If Job had not been so pre occupied in the defense of his self-righteous piety and his three friends were ministering Godly love, grace, mercy and compassion towards him, his spirit would have leaped with overwhelming joy from the repentance of a contrite heart.

(Job 32) *Then Elihu son of Barakel the Buzite, of the clan of Ram, became angry. He was angry because Job refused to* *admit that he had sinned and that God was right in punishing him. He was also angry with Job's three friends because they had condemned God by their inability to answer Job's arguments. Elihu had waited for the others to speak because they were older than he. But when he saw that they had no further reply, he spoke out angrily. Elihu said, I am young and you are old, so I held back and did not dare to tell you what I think. I thought, those who are older should speak, for wisdom comes with age. Surely it is God's Spirit within people, the breath of the Almighty within them that makes them intelligent. But sometimes the elders are not wise. Sometimes the aged do not understand justice. So listen to me and let me express my opinion. I have waited all this time, listening very carefully to your arguments, listening to you grope for words. I have listened, but not one of you has refuted Job or answered his arguments. And don't tell me, he is too wise for us. Only God can convince him. If Job had been arguing with me, I would not answer with that kind of logic! You sit there baffled, with no further response. Should I continue to wait, now that you are silent? Must I also remain silent? No, I will say my piece. I will speak my mind. I surely will. For I am pent up and full of words, and the spirit within me urges me on. I am like a wine cask without a vent. My words are ready to burst out! I must speak to find relief, so let me give my answers. I won't play favorites or try to flatter anyone. And if I tried, my Creator would soon do away with me.*

*(**Job 33**) Listen, Job, to what I have to say. Now that I have begun to speak, let me continue. I speak with all sincerity; I speak the truth. For the Spirit of God has made me, and the breath of the Almighty gives me life. Answer me, if you can; make your case and take your stand. Look, you and I are the same before God. I, too, was formed from clay. So you don't need to be afraid of me. I am not some great person to make you nervous and afraid. You have said it in my hearing. I have heard your very words. You said, I*

am pure; I am innocent; I have not sinned. God is picking a quarrel with me and he considers me to be his enemy. He puts my feet in the stocks and watches every move I make.

In this you are not right, and I will show you why. As you yourself have said, God is greater than any person. So why are you bringing a charge against him? You say, He does not respond to people's complaints. But God speaks again and again, though people do not recognize it. He speaks in dreams, in visions of the night when deep sleep falls on people as they lie in bed. He whispers in their ear and terrifies them with his warning. He causes them to change their minds; he keeps them from pride. He keeps them from the grave, from crossing over the river of death.

Or God disciplines people [through the consequences of breaking His Laws] *with sickness and pain, with ceaseless aching in their bones. They lose their appetite and do not care for even the most delicious food. They waste away to skin and bones. They are at death's door; the angels of death wait for them. But if a **special messenger*** [Jesus Christ the Messiah?] *from heaven is there to intercede for a person, to declare that he is upright, God will be gracious and say, set him free. Do not make him die, for I have found a ransom for his life. Then his body will become as healthy as a child's, firm and youthful again. When he prays to God, he will be accepted. And God will receive him with joy and restore him to good standing.*

He will declare to his friends, I sinned, but it was not worth it. God rescued me from the grave, and now my life is filled with light. Yes, God often does these things for people. He rescues them from the grave so they may live in the light of the living. Mark this well, Job. Listen to me, and let me say more. But if you have anything to say, go ahead. I want to hear it, for I am anxious to see you justified. But if not, then listen to me. Keep silent and I will teach you wisdom!

Listen to me, you wise men. Pay attention, you who have knowledge. Just as the mouth tastes good food, the ear tests the words it hears. So let us discern for ourselves what is right; let us learn together what is good. For Job has said, I am innocent, but God has taken away my rights. I am innocent, but they call me a liar. My suffering is incurable, even though I have not sinned. Has there ever been a man as arrogant as Job, with his thirst for irreverent talk?

He seeks the companionship of evil people. He spends his time with wicked men. He has even said, why waste time trying to please God? Listen to me, you who have understanding. Everyone knows that God doesn't sin! The Almighty can do no wrong. He repays people according to their deeds. He treats people according to their ways. There is no truer statement than this: God will not do wrong. The Almighty cannot twist justice. Who put the world in His care? Who has set the whole world in place? If God were to take back His spirit and withdraw His breath, all life would cease, and humanity would turn again to dust.

Listen now and try to understand. Could God govern if he hated justice? Are you going to condemn the almighty Judge? For he says to kings and nobles, you are wicked and unjust. He doesn't care how great a person may be, and he doesn't pay any more attention to the rich than to the poor. He made them all. In a moment they die. At midnight they all pass away; the mighty are removed without human hand. For God carefully watches the way people live; He sees everything they do. No darkness is thick enough to hide the wicked from His eyes. For it is not up to mortals to decide when to come before God in judgment.

He brings the mighty to ruin without asking anyone, and He sets up others in their places. He watches what they do, and in the night He overturns them, destroying them. He openly strikes them down for their wickedness. For they no longer follow him. They have no respect for any of his ways.

So they cause the poor to cry out, catching God's attention. Yes, He hears the cries of the needy. When He is quiet, who can make trouble? But when He hides his face, who can find Him? He prevents the godless from ruling so they cannot be a snare to the people.

Elihu suggests a solution for preventing the majority of Job's grief ... and maybe ours:

Why don't people say to God, I have sinned, but I will sin no more? Or I don't know what evil I have done; tell me, and I will stop at once. Must God tailor His justice to your demands? But you have rejected him! The choice is yours, not mine. Go ahead; share your wisdom with us. After all, bright people will tell me, and wise people will hear me say, **Job speaks without knowledge; his words lack insight.** *Job, you deserve the maximum penalty for the wicked way you have talked. For now you have added rebellion and blasphemy against God to your other sins.*

Job 36 *Elihu continued speaking: Let me go on, and I will show you the truth of what I am saying. For I have not finished defending God! I will give you many illustrations of the righteousness of my Creator. I am telling you the honest truth, for I am a man of well-rounded knowledge. God is mighty, yet he does not despise anyone! He is mighty in both power and understanding. He does not let the wicked live but gives justice to the afflicted.*

His eyes never leave the innocent, but He establishes and exalts them with kings forever. If troubles come upon them and they are enslaved and afflicted, He takes the trouble to show them the reason [their thoughts and the words of their mouth]. *He shows them their sins, for they have behaved proudly. He gets their attention and says they must turn away from evil. If they listen and obey God, then they will be blessed with prosperity throughout their lives. All their years will be pleasant. But if they refuse to listen to Him, they will perish in battle and die from lack of understanding.* [**Hosea**

4:6 *My people are destroyed for lack of knowledge: because you have rejected knowledge, I will also reject you.*]

For the godless are full of resentment. Even when He punishes them, they refuse to cry out to Him for help. They die young after wasting their lives in immoral living. But by means of their suffering, He rescues those who suffer. For He gets their attention through adversity [from the adversary Satan]. *God has led you away from danger, giving you freedom. You have prospered in a wide and pleasant valley. But you are too obsessed with judgment on the godless. Don't worry, justice will be upheld. But watch out, or you may be seduced with wealth.*

Don't let yourself be bribed into sin [by Satan, not God]. *Could all your wealth and mighty efforts keep you from distress? Do not long for the cover of night, for that is when people will be destroyed. Be on guard! Turn back from evil, for it was to prevent you from getting into a life of evil that God sent this suffering.* [Jesus said, **John 10:10** *The thief cometh not, but for to steal, and to kill, and to destroy: I am come that they might have life, and that they might have it more abundantly.*] *Look, God is all-powerful. Who is a teacher like him? No one can tell Him what to do. No one can say to Him, You have done wrong. Instead, glorify His mighty works, singing songs of praise. Everyone has seen these things, but only from a distance.*

Job was beginning to realize that whenever we justify ourselves, we condemn God. **Psalms 51:4** *Against You, You only, have I sinned, and done this evil in Your sight: that You might be justified when You speak, and be clear when You judge.* But, on the other hand, when we condemn ourselves, we are justifing God. *Wisdom is justified of all her children.* This is a grand point. The truly broken and contrite heart will vindicate God, not ourselves, at all cost. *Let God be true, but every man a liar; as it is written, that you might be justified in your sayings, and might overcome when you are judged.*

(**Romans 3: 4**) It is true wisdom to judge yourself and justify Him. The very moment we humble our soul in self-judgment, God rises before it in all the majesty of His grace as the Justifier. However, as long as we are ruled by a spirit of self-righteousness and self-vindication or self-complacency, we will be blind to and strangers of God's Grace, Mercy and Righteousness.

Job was still blindly headed down the road to destruction when Elihu started throwing up detour signs and warning signs to indicate that he was on the wrong road: repent, turn around and go the other way! My dear friend, consider this: Are you on the road of self-righteousness, self-vindication and self-complacency? If so, please realize it is the road to self-destruction. God isn't destroying you, your family or your possessions; it is Satan who is destroying you, and you are the one giving him permission to do so by the very words of your own mouth. For you to simply be warned is not enough, you need to know where to turn and why.

This book will aid in pointing out the possible and definite hazards along the way and what is needed for the journey. If you have not put your trust and faith in Jesus Christ, you are presently on that road to destruction. **Matthew 7:13-14** *You can enter God's Kingdom only through the narrow gate. The highway to hell is broad, and its gate is wide for the many who choose the easy way. But the gateway to life is small, and the road is narrow, and only a few ever find it.* **John 14:6** *Jesus told him, I am the way, the truth, and the life. No one can come to the Father except through me.*

Sinners need to be told that there is only one road that leads to eternal life, the one that leads to a contrite heart and genuine repentance. That road is paved with humility and at its end there is nothing but that pure and precious Grace of God and the forgiveness and healing that comes through Jesus Christ our Lord. Please hear me! There is nothing but wrath and death for the self-righteous — nothing but grace and life for the self-judged. After listening to Job's rant, we may understand why Elihu's wrath was kindled against him. Elihu was entirely on God's side. Job was not. We hear nothing of Elihu until Job 32, though it is very evident that he had been an attentive listener to the whole discussion. He had patiently listened to both sides, and he found both wrong. Job was wrong in seeking to defend himself; and his friends were wrong to condemn him.

How often is this scenario played out in confrontations and controversies? We take turns condemning each other or defending ourselves. A little brokenness on one side, or a little softness on the other, would go a long way towards settling misunderstandings and strife. This is not the case when we are dealing with God's truth. In that case one must be bold, decisive, and unyielding. To yield or apologize where the truth of God or the glory of Jesus Christ is concerned would mean disloyalty to the One to whom we owe everything. He did not hesitate to sacrifice everything including His life to secure our place in glory.

If we are expressing a claim or proclamation of our Lord, we should never balk or shrink back with timidity, but speak with the authority He imparted to those who believe. God forbid we should water down the Gospel for fear of offending someone or to appear seeker friendly. **Psalms 119:165** *Great peace have they which love your law: and nothing shall offend them.* **Ephesians 6:10-20** *Be strong in the Lord, and in the power of His might. Put on the whole armor of God, that you may be able to stand against the wiles of the devil. For we wrestle not against flesh and blood, but against principalities, against powers, against the rulers of the darkness of this world, against spiritual wickedness in high places. Wherefore take unto you the whole armor of God that ye may be able to withstand in the evil day, and having done all, to stand. Stand therefore, having your loins girt about with truth, and having on the breastplate of righteousness; and* *your feet shod with the preparation of the gospel of peace; above all, taking the shield of faith, wherewith ye shall be able to quench all the fiery darts of the wicked. And take the helmet of salvation, and the sword of the Spirit, which is the word of God: Praying always with all prayer and supplication in the Spirit, and watching thereunto with all perseverance and supplication for all saints; and for me, that utterance may be given unto me, that I may open my mouth boldly, to make known the mystery of the gospel, For which I am an ambassador in bonds: that therein I may speak boldly, as I ought to speak.*

Paul was not ashamed of the Gospel nor did he ever shrink back; rather he *opened his mouth boldly* that his *speech and his preaching was not with enticing words of man's wisdom, but in demonstration of the Spirit and of power: That your faith should not stand in the wisdom of men, but in the power of God.* **1Corinthians 2:4-5**

Paul also proclaimed: *I once thought all these things were so very important, but now I consider them worthless because of what Christ has done. Yes, everything else is worthless when compared with the priceless gain of knowing Christ Jesus my Lord and for what his crucifixion and personal sacrifice means to me. I have disregarded everything else, counting it all as dung, compared to knowing Jesus Christ and becoming one with him. I no longer count on my own goodness or my ability to obey God's law, but I trust Christ Jesus to save me. For God's way of making us right with Himself depends only on faith. As a result, I can truly know Him and experience the mighty power that raised Him from the dead. I can learn what it means to suffer with Him, sharing in his death, so that, somehow, I can experience that resurrection power!* **Philippians 3:8-11**

Much like the dedication of Paul to the service of God through Christ, there is something divinely striking and prevalent in the ministry of Elihu. He mirrors the divine righteousness of God as opposed to Job's three friends. His name is translated "God is he," which leads us to believe he was a type of our Lord Jesus Christ, sent to show Job the truth and reveal God's Light, such as He did in delivering the Truth and Light of the new covenant in taking our place by dying for our sins.

He brings God into the picture, stopping the mouths of both Job and his friends. Elihu never mentions experience, appeals to tradition, or wields the hammer of legality; he simply shares the law, justice, divinity and mercy of God. This is the only way to squelch strife and dissolve controversy, stopping the mouth, and ending the war of words. **Romans 3:19** *Now we know that whatever the law says, it says to those who are under the law, that **every mouth may be stopped**, and **all the world** may become **guilty before God**. Therefore by the deeds of the law no flesh will be justified in His sight, for **by the law is the knowledge of sin**.* **Psalms 19:7** *For the **law of the Lord is perfect converting the soul**.*

When Elihu saw that *there was no answer* in the mouth of these three men, his wrath was kindled. In all their reasonings, and arguments, in all their references to experience, tradition, and legality, still there was "no answer." Job's friends had said many true things, made many feeble attempts using many vain words to convince Job of the error of his ways; *and a fool's voice is known by his many words* (**Ecclesiastes 5:3**), but be it carefully noted, they found "no answer." A heart that is not regenerated or contrite is quick to give an answer or reply. *Wherefore, my beloved brethren, let every man be swift to hear, slow to speak, slow to wrath* (**James 1:19**) *... for they think that they shall be heard for their much speaking* (**Matthew 6:7**). Yet, Job's friends found "no answer." And Elihu answered and said, *I am young, and you are very old; wherefore I was afraid, and dared not show my opinion. I said, let experience speak first...they either do not speak at all, or they speak a quantity of error and folly,* *and I would have thought that a multitude of years should teach wisdom. But there is a spirit in man; and the inspiration of the Almighty gives him understanding.*

No sooner does Elihu speak that everyone's mouths are stopped. We are listening to a man that knows God personally—a man who is righteous and just, one who stands in God's Divine presence. It is not a man speaking with the enticing words of man's wisdom drawn from his own wretched, self-centered, self-righteous, one-sided experience; nor is it a man appealing to an elusive, shady, questionable antiquity, or to pathetic traditions, or the ever conflicting and contradicting voices of the many self-absorbed fathers. *For laying aside the commandment of God, you hold the tradition of men, as the washing of pots and cups: and many other such like things you do.* (**Mark 7:8**) *Beware lest any man spoil you through philosophy and vain deceit, after the tradition of men, after the rudiments of the world, and not after Christ.* (**Colossians 2:8**)

No, we have before us a diligent, faithful, bold ambassador *approved to God a worker who does not need to be ashamed, rightly dividing the word of truth.* (**2Timothy 2:15**) who invites us into the very presence of "the inspiration of the Almighty," our Judge and Deliverer.

Great men are not always wise; neither do the aged understand judgment. (**Job 32:9**) It is quite obvious at this point that Elihu has not come to judge or condemn Job, but to correct and encourage. He simply tells Job the truth; he rebukes, but does not punish him. Elihu manifests the power of "the still small voice"— he soul-soothing, heart-melting virtue of Godly Grace. Job has voiced many self-righteous opinions about himself, and his self-proclaimed innocence had sprouted from a root of pride to which the Word of Truth had to be applied. For the Word of God *is quick and powerful, and sharper than any two-edged sword, piercing even to the dividing asunder of soul and spirit, and of the joints and* *marrow, and is a discerner of the thoughts and intents of the heart.* (**Hebrews 4:12**) *Surely,* says Elihu, *you have spoken in my hearing, and I have heard the voice of your words, saying, "I am clean, without transgression, I am innocent; neither is there iniquity in me."*

Such words for any mortal sinner to utter! Surely, though, "the true light" in which Job should walk did not shine into every corner of his soul. You might marvel at such a matter-of-fact profession of innocence. And yet notice what Job says. Although he professes to be so clean, so innocent, so free from iniquity, he feels free to judge God by assuming his trials and tribulations are from Him. Here he hurls three of his total of 77 false charges against God such as: *He finds occasions to count me for His enemy. He puts my feet in the stocks, He marks all my paths.* Here is a blatant discrepancy. How could a holy, just, and righteous Being count a pure and innocent man His enemy? Impossible! Either Job was deceived, or God was unrighteous; and it isn't long before Elihu, the prophet from God, is pronouncing a judgment and telling us which is which. *Behold, in this thou art not just: I will answer you, that God is greater than man.* What a simple truth! And yet how often misunderstood! If God is greater than man, then, obviously, He and not man must be the Judge of what is right. This is what the corrupt, deceitful, infidel heart refuses to accept, hence the constant tendency to sit in judgment upon the works and ways and Word of God—upon God Himself. Man, in his fallen and sinful nature, pronounces judgment upon the worthiness and righteousness of God, to decide upon what God should and shouldn't say or do. He proves himself utterly ignorant of that most simple, obvious, necessary truth, that *God is greater than man.* So who is right, Job or God? Job is now, where we all end up at one time or another, at the end of our rope! This is the place where you have only two choices: Form the end of the rope into a hangman's noose or let go and let God!

CHAPTER 8

Justification, Repentance or Judgment?

What I am about to share with you should give you great hope and much joy. Looking back over the account of Job's life, you read what appears to be one of history's most unlikely, unqualified candidates for receiving the wrath of God. The big question is, did he receive God's wrath? Before answering that question, answer this one. What was God's opinion of Job's character? Let me help you out: **Job 1:8** *And the Lord God said unto Satan, Hast thou considered my servant Job, that there is none like him in the earth, a perfect and an upright man, one that fears God, and shuns evil?* Now let me get this straight, God is perfect, his judgment is perfect and righteous, and He judges Job to be perfect and upright. Could this same God now be entering into a wager or bet with Satan, or even allowing this vile, disgusting being to test Job or orchestrate a trial against him? I beg you to appeal, just for a moment, to the God-given wisdom and your Godly sense. Let go of the adopted, preconceived religious and worldly-motivated paradigms and notions that you have held onto most of your life.

Could you trust a God that says one thing and demonstrates the opposite? Remember, this is the God that said: *"I am the LORD that heals you." "God is not the God of the dead, but of the living," "Fear thou not; for I* [am] *with you: be not dismayed; for I* [am] *your God: I will strengthen you; yea, I will help you; yea, I will uphold you with the right hand of my righteousness." "But I am poor and needy; yet the Lord thinks upon me: thou* [art] *my help and my deliverer; make no tarrying, O my God." "And I will give you the treasures of darkness, and hidden riches of secret places, that thou may know that I, the LORD, which call you by your name, am the God of Israel." "I am the LORD your God which teaches you to profit, which leads you by the way that thou should go." "And I will give them a heart to know me, that I am the LORD: and they shall be my people, and I will be their God: for they shall return unto me with their whole heart." "Behold, this day I am going the way of all the earth: and ye know in all your hearts and in all your souls, that not one thing hath failed of all the good things which the LORD your God spoke concerning you; all are come to pass unto you, and not one thing hath failed thereof."* Do these describe a God that will call a man just, upright, God-fearing and a man that shuns evil, and then puts a trial or test on him by killing his family, destroying all his possessions and racking his body with disease from head to foot? Satan wants you to believe that! He had Job believing it!

When the opinions of a respected man like Matthew Henry, author, Bible teacher, minister, theologian and college professor, are revered by seminary students, pastor, preachers and evangelist, and they read his commentaries like they are the gospel, is it any wonder that very few believe God's will is for us to be healed and stay healed? Henry not only believed that God gave Satan the go-ahead to kill Job's family and destroy all he owned, but he twisted the scripture by claiming God said, "All that he has is in your hand, make the trial as sharp as thou canst and do your worst at him." That is not true! Any believer that reads that would realize that God could possibly do the same thing to them and, if so, how could they ever believe God for healing if it was His will that they be sick? Henry says, "God does this for His own glory..."; so how could they possibly ask Him to heal them or to ask others to pray that He would, for they would be going against or usurping God's will for your life?

However, I have prayed for you, Peter that your faith should not fail. **Luke 22:31-32** Henry goes on to say that he desired Job to be tried as He wished Peter to be "sifted," but took care that his faith should not fail. That is not the case; Jesus did not give Satan permission to sift Peter, any more than He did for him to sift Job, but simply told Peter that Satan wanted to have him that he might sift him like wheat. Could it be that when our faith fails, we open the door to Satan's attacks, by the confessions of our mouth through our lack of faith? *Without faith it is impossible to please God.*

Matthew Henry in his commentary on Job misquotes the following scripture: *...only upon him, put forth not your hand.* Henry twists the scripture to say, "Meddle not with his body, but only with his estate." All God said was, *All that Job has is in your power;* God didn't say a word giving permission to meddle with anything! He was only stating an observation. When Satan returned to God after wreaking havoc on Job's family and property, Satan suggested that if God would stretch forth his hand and touch his flesh, Job would curse Him to His face. Henry suggested God changed His mind and now let Satan touch his flesh. Again, not true; God was simply making another observation that something must have happened since the last conversation between them that gave Satan access to Job's flesh. What could have changed or happened to allow that? Could it be all the negative confessions and accusations spewing from Job's mouth? From out of the abundance of his fear-filled heart, his mouth speaks.

For example: *The Lord gives and the Lord takes away... I'm cursed from my birth... Shouldn't we receive good and evil from God?*

After each terrible event caused by Satan, he always made sure he spared one servant to be a messenger of evil tidings to tell Job, in order to strike fear in his heart. See **Job 1:14, 1:16, 1:17, 1:18. Psalms 112:7** says, *He shall not be afraid of evil tidings...but keep his heart fixed, trusting in the Lord.* **Proverbs 4:23-4** *Keep your heart with all diligence, for out of it are the issues of life. Put away from you a deeitful mouth and perverse lips put far from you.*

Proverbs 4:20 *Attend to my words* [not Satan's], *incline your ears unto my sayings and keep them in the midst of your heart, they are health to all those that find them and health to all their flesh.* Satan's words, "evil tidings" are **death** to those that find them and **sickness and disease** to all their flesh.

As Job had finally cried out to God, requesting to be shown the error of his ways and to reveal to him his sin, God answered his prayers and sent him a savior, Elihu—just like God did for us by sending His only begotten Son Jesus, who brought us salvation for the remittance of sin, that whosoever believes in Him will not perish, but have everlasting life. By the time Elihu has finished exhorting Job and pointing out his sin and transgressions against God, Job was ready for an encounter with God. As you recall, Job made 77 false accusations against God and basically blamed Him for all his calamity, which went on for many chapters. Job finally recognized that maybe his mouth could be the source of most, if not all his problems. Elihu was responsible for Job's revelation by describing God's majesty, greatness, righteousness, justice, mercy, grace, fairness, and unwarranted favor and forgiveness.

By the end of chapter 39, Job is pretty much wrung out, humbled and undone, at the end of himself, where most people have to be to finally realize they need God. They acknowledge that they can no longer do it on their own, the weight of sin has taken its toll, and they realize life without God is meaningless and vain.

Then the Lord said to Job, *Do you still want to argue with the Almighty? You are God's critic, but do you have the answers?* Then Job replied to the Lord, *I am nothing, how could I ever find the answers? I will put my hand over my mouth in silence. I have said too much already. I have nothing more to say.* He finally realizes the power in the tongue!

God reveals to Job what the source was that opened up the protective hedge around him and his family. Fear unlocked the door and self-righteousness turned the knob. God asked him in **Job 40:8** Are *you going to discredit my justice and condemn me so you can say you are right?*

God rebuked Job for the next two chapters and in **42:3** he acknowledges the root cause of his calamities: *You ask, "Who is this that questions my wisdom with such ignorance?" It is I. And I was talking about things I did not understand, things far too wonderful for me."* **Hosea 4:6** *My people are destroyed* [by whom, God or Satan?] *for lack of knowledge: because you have rejected knowledge."*

Elihu was the messenger of that knowledge. Until Job realized his words were producing negative results and were giving Satan permission to kill, steal and destroy, he was powerless, and God was powerless to help him, because Job had a free will to choose his own course by the power of his words. His words were fear-filled, not faith-filled. However, if we will confess our sins, God is faithful and just to forgive us of our sins and cleanse us of all unrighteousness. If we acknowledge our sin and repent, God can then restore what the thief has killed, stolen or destroyed. **Joel 2:25** *And I will restore to you the years that the locust hath eaten, the cankerworm, and the caterpillar, and the palmerworm have destroyed..."* That is exactly what Job did.

*You said, Listen and I will speak! I have some questions for you, and you must answer them. I had heard about you before, but now **I have seen you with my own eyes**. I take back everything I said, and **I sit in dust and ashes to show my repentance.**"* Unlike Job, his friends saw no need to repent for their actions; however God thought differently!

After the Lord had finished speaking to Job, he said to Eliphaz: "I am angry with you and with your two friends, for you have not been right in what you said about Me, as my servant Job was. Now take seven young bulls and seven rams and go to My servant Job and offer a burnt offering for yourselves. My servant Job will pray for you, and I will accept his prayer on your behalf. I will not treat you as you deserve, for you have not been right in what you said about Me, as my servant Job was." So Eliphaz, Bildad, and Zophar did as the Lord commanded them, and the Lord accepted Job's prayer. When Job prayed for his friends, the Lord restored his fortunes. In fact, the Lord gave him twice as much as before! If Job had repented in Chapter 1 verse 14, when Satan took his oxen and donkeys, he would have slammed the door in Satan's face and the hedge would have been restored along with Job's right-standing with God! Is there a lesson in this somewhere for us? I pray, several.

A major spiritual truth and lesson is learning to guard your words, and hiding God's Word in your heart and knowing whom to fear: *But I will forewarn you whom you shall fear: Fear him, which after he has killed has power to cast into hell; yes, I say unto you, Fear him.* **Luke 12:5**

CHAPTER 9

Is Job's God Your God?

I hope that as you read the chapter, "Job Said, But God Said," you noticed how Job's past and present experiences, personal view of life, the influences of others on him, and spiritual views formed by positive and negative interaction with others, all played a role in programming, shaping and forming Job's opinions, outlook on life, and moral values and judgments. Do our daily encounters with life's challenges and blessings influence the way we perceive God and how strong our faith will be in that God? How many times have you heard someone say, "My God wouldn't do this or that," or "what kind of a God would do this or that?" Why does God allow wars or sickness and disease, murders, rapes and abortion?

If it is true that each person's perception of God can be largely attributed to their life experiences, both good and bad, that would mean that, with the exception of believers (followers of Jesus Christ), everyone has a different concept and belief of who God is and what He does or does not do. Volcanic island dwellers believe in a fire god or possibly several, such as the sun god, god of the sea, god of the wind and rain, and so on. Various jungle tribes may worship separate gods, one the tiger, another the great ape, another the elephant, and it could have all started by a family member becoming the lunch of an animal, or in Greece a victim of the sea (Neptune or Poseidon) or a lightning bolt (Thor) .

The God of the Bible, referred to as the God of Abraham, Isaac and Jacob, is the only God that preserved a detailed, written record of his character, nature, precepts, statutes and laws. This God, the Hebrew God of Abraham, Isaac and Jacob (Israel), is called by many names.

- Jehovah - The Lord - Exodus 6:2-3
- Jehovah-Adon Kal Ha'arets- Lord of Earth - Joshua 3:13
- Jehovah-Bara - Lord Creator - Isaiah 40:28
- Jehovah-Chatsahi - Lord my Strength - Psalm 27:1
- Jehovah-Chereb - Lord the Sword - Deuteronomy 33:29
- Jehovah-Eli - Lord my God - Psalm 18:2
- Jehovah-Elyon - Lord Most High - Psalm 38:2
- Jehovah-Gador Milchamah - Mighty in Battle - Psalm 24:8
- Jehovah-Ganan - Lord Our Defense - Psalm 89:18
- Jehovah-Go'el - Lord My Redeemer - Isaiah 49:26, 60:16
- Jehovah-Hamelech - Lord King - Psalm 98:6
- Jehovah-Hashopet - Lord My Judge - Judges 6:27
- Jehovah-Helech 'Olam - Lord King Forever- Psalm 10:16
- Jehovah-Hoshe'ah - Lord Saves - Psalm 20:9
- Jehovah-Jireh - Provider - Gen. 22:14, I John 4:9, Philippians 4:19
- Jehovah-Kabodhi - Lord my Glory - Psalm 3:3
- Jehovah-Kanna - Lord Jealous - Exodus 34:14
- Jehovah-Keren-Yish'i - Horn of Salvation - Psalm 18:2
- Jehovah-M'Kaddesh - Sanctifier - I Corinthians 1:30

- Jehovah-Machsi - Lord my Refuge - Psalm 91:9
- Jehovah-Magen - Lord my Shield -
  Deuteronomy 33:29
- Jehovah-Ma'oz - Lord my Fortress - Jeremiah 16:19
- Jehovah-Mephalti - Lord my Deliverer - Psalm 18:2
- Jehovah-Metshodhathi - Lord my Fortress -
  Psalm 18:2
- Jehovah-Misqabbi - Lord my High Tower -
  Psalm 18:2
- Jehovah-M'gaddishcem - Lord my Sanctifier -
  Exodus 31:13
- Jehovah-Naheh - Lord who Smites - Ezekiel 7:9
- Jehovah-Nissi - Banner - I Chronicles 29:11-13
- Jehovah-Rohi - Shepherd - Psalm 23
- Jehovah-Rophe - Healer - Isaiah 53:4,5
- Jehovah-Sabaoth - Lord of Hosts - I Samuel 1:3
- Jehovah-Sel'i - Lord my Rock - Psalm 18:2
- Jehovah-Shalom - Peace - Isaiah 9:6,
  Romans 8:31-35
- Jehovah-Shammah - Present - Hebrews 13:5
- Jehovah-Tsidkenu - Righteousness -
  I Corinthians 1:30
- Jehovah-Tsori - Lord my Strength - Psalm 19:14
- Jehovah-Yeshua - Lord my Savior - Isaiah 49:26
- Jehovah-'Ez-Lami - Lord my Strength - Psalm 28:7
- Jehovah-'Immeku - Lord Is With You - Judges 6:12
- Jehovah-'Izoa Hakaboth - Lord Strong -Mighty -
  Psalm 24:8
- Jehovah-'Ori - Lord my Light - Psalm 27:1
- Jehovah-'Uzam - Lord Strength in Trouble -
  Isaiah 49:26; Psalm 37:39

There are over 600 individual names for God referenced in the Bible, with every name describing God's Holiness, Righteousness, Grace, Mercy, Justice, Fairness, Sovereignty,

Omnipresence, Omniscience, Perfection, Majesty, Power, Might, Divinity, Ever-lasting, the Beginning and the End, Alpha and Omega... All in All.

According to Wikipedia, Hinduism is the oldest religion dating back to the Bronze Age (approximately 1500 BCE). It is the world's third largest religion following Christianity and Islam. With close to a billion adherents, Hinduism involves a choice to worship in excess of 330 million gods and goddesses. They seem to have created a god for every emotion, feeling, concept, living creature and inanimate object known to man.

Enough about gods with a little "g". Let's not get sidetracked by giving our attention over to vain, worthless topics or discussions. I will get straight to the point by asking this poignant question: Who or what is your god? Do you have a personal relationship with him, her or it? If your god is mother nature, then I guess the answer to having a personal relationship would be no. You ask why did I pick nature first, out of the billions of other possibilities for gods, to worship and adore.

I'm glad you asked! Let me answer that with **Romans 1:18-32** (New Living Testament):

18. But God shows His anger from heaven against all sinful, wicked people who push the truth away from themselves. 19. For the truth about God is known to them instinctively. God has put this knowledge in their hearts. 20. From the time the world was created, people have seen the earth and sky and all that God made. They can clearly see His invisible qualities—His eternal power and divine nature. So they have no excuse whatsoever for not knowing God.

21. Yes, they knew God, but they wouldn't worship him as God or even give Him thanks. And they began to think up foolish ideas of what God was like. The result was that their minds became dark and confused. 22. Claiming to be wise, they became utter fools instead. 23. And instead of worshiping the glorious, ever-living God, they worshiped idols made to look like mere people, or birds and animals and snakes.

24. So God let them go ahead and do whatever shameful things their hearts desired. As a result, they did vile and degrading things with each other's bodies. 25. Instead of believing what they knew was the truth about God, they deliberately chose to believe lies. So they worshiped the things God made but not the Creator himself, who is to be praised forever. Amen.

26. That is why God abandoned them to their shameful desires. Even the women turned against the natural way to have sex and instead indulged in sex with each other. 27. And the men, instead of having normal sexual relationships with women, burned with lust for each other. Men did shameful things with other men and, as a result, suffered within themselves the penalty they so richly deserved.

28. When they refused to acknowledge God, He abandoned them to their evil minds and let them do things that should never be done. 29. Their lives became full of every kind of wickedness, sin, greed, hate, envy, murder, fighting, deception, malicious behavior, and gossip. 30. They are backstabbers, haters of God, insolent, proud, and boastful. They are forever inventing new ways of sinning and are disobedient to their parents. 31. They refuse to understand, break their promises, and are heartless and unforgiving. 32. They are fully aware of God's death penalty for those who do these things, yet they go right ahead and do them anyway. And, worse yet, they encourage others to do them, too.

So now you know why I chose nature first. Most people have decided to worship the creation rather than the Creator. You cannot have a close personal relationship with the creation! Does nature provide love and compassion, wise counsel, does it provide all your needs, clothes, daily bread, healing, protection, or the ultimate, life after death?

So tell me, did your god create you and everything your eyes can and cannot see? If so, does your god have rules to live by or does he or she just allow you to live your life how you please, with little no consequences? If we finite, mortal humans have subscribed to creating laws and rules to live under, how much more would an all-powerful, all-knowing, wise, righteous, holy God require the same or more. I have never met anyone that considered God's Ten Commandments to be burdensome or unfair. On the contrary, God's laws not only protect the quality of our lives individually, but they afford protection and peace of mind as a society. For the purpose of this illustration, I will assume that you have never read the Bible, darkened the door of a church, listened to the words of a Christmas carol, or watched a Billy Graham crusade. Or that you basically know nothing about Judeo-Christian doctrine or theology.

I will now proceed to give you an outline of the Bible: God created the heavens and the earth, Adam and Eve disobeyed God (sinned), received the penalty: death and hell. God made a way to keep us from going to hell by having His Son die for us, taking our sin upon Himself. What is more, it is a free gift; we can't earn salvation, we can only receive it by faith and place our trust and faith in Jesus Christ, God's Son. This God calls receiving salvation the second birth or being born again (of the spirit) so we can spend an eternity in heaven with Him.

You now boldly proclaim, "I could not serve a God that sends people to hell. My god would never send anyone to hell!" Okay, let's take a look at this proclamation. **1.** Where did you learn about your god? **2.** Was it a religious cult that was started by a man or a woman that claims we can all become like God or become gods ourselves? **3.** Was it a religion that promises you a house full of virgins if you die while killing women, innocent babies and children in the name of a god? **4.** Is your god found in the trees, rocks, water, sky and universe, and does he give you a nice warm fuzzy feeling of oneness with everything? **5.** Does your god have rules or laws to govern your life? **6.** Can you or do you have a personal relationship with your god? **7.** Can you willfully lie, steal, use God's name in vain, commit adultery, covet, murder, blaspheme, serve other gods, dishonor your parents, not put God first and not expect to be punished?

You have a free will to serve God or not, to love God or not, to steal or not, to lie or not, to take a life or not. If you choose to do any of these things, are you not also choosing the consequences of your choice? So, if the penalty is hell, is God sending you there, or is it **your** choice to go by choosing to break His law?

You can choose to believe or not to believe in this God; it is your free will. Just remember three facts: **1.** If you choose not to believe in a just and righteous God, it does not change the facts. **2.** You will not be standing in front of the god you created in your mind because that god is a figment of your imagination, a god you made up in your mind for convenience, a fantasy or imagery. The god you dreamed up in your brain allows you to do what you want without any consequences. **3.** This made-up god in your head is not the One you will be standing in front of on Judgment Day. You will be standing before the Judge of Abraham, Isaac and Jacob and you will be without excuse because I just told you the truth.

Because God is holy and righteous, He cannot and will not tolerate sin of any kind. So, therefore, because He is a just and righteous Judge, He has no choice but to pass righteous judgment upon us. Since the wages of sin is death, we must pay the price. However, *God so loved the world that he gave His only begotten Son, that whosoever believes in Him, shall not perish, but have everlasting life. For God did not send His Son into the world to condemn the world, but that the world through Him might be saved* (**John 3:16-17**).

Now this is eternal life, that they may know You, the only true God, and Jesus Christ whom You have sent (**John 17:3**).

You may ask, "How can I know God?" We can know God through His Word (the Bible). The Bible reveals God's character, nature and purpose for mankind. It is through reading His Word that we come to knowledge of the righteousness of God and what He requires from us.

What is it that separates us from the presence of God and knowing Him intimately? Our sin has come between us and God — it prevents us from knowing Him personally and experiencing His love. God's Word says, *All have sinned and fall short of the glory of God* (**Romans 3:23**). Man was created to have fellowship with God, but because of his sin (i.e., breaking God's Law) he is separated from Him.

The wages of sin is death (**Romans 6:23a**). The ultimate result of this death is an eternity in hell. This spiritual death results in separation from God. Man is sinful and God is holy. This creates a gulf between God and man. Jesus becomes an intercessor and bridges that gulf.

God sacrificed His Son to pay the price for our sin. *God demonstrated His own love toward us, in that while we were still sinners, Christ died for us* (**Romans 5:8**). *He died in our place; He who knew no sin became sin for us. This removed our burden of sin and allows us to enter into that desired fellowship if we follow His way. He is the only way. Jesus said, I am the way, the truth, and the life. No one comes to the Father except through Me* (**John 14:6**).

It is not enough for you to know these truths; you must place your trust in Jesus Christ as your personal Lord and Savior. It is by repenting of our sins and believing on Christ and placing your total trust and faith in Him that you will come to know God personally and experience His love.

But as many as receive Him, to them He gave the right to become children of God, to those who believe in His name (**John 1:12**). *For by grace you have been saved through* *faith, and that not of yourselves; it is the gift of God, not of works, lest anyone should boast. For we are His workmanship, created in Christ Jesus for good works, which God prepared beforehand that we should walk in them* (**Ephesians 2:8-10**).

Repent, and let every one of you be baptized in the name of Jesus Christ for the remission of sins; and you shall receive the gift of the Holy Spirit (**Acts 2:38**). You can receive Jesus Christ right now by faith. *If you confess with your mouth the Lord Jesus and believe in your heart that God has raised Him from the dead, you will be saved. For with the heart, one believes unto righteousness, and with the mouth confession is made to salvation* (**Romans 10:9-10**).

I pray you will make that decision to surrender your heart and soul to Jesus Christ today—and if you already have, welcome to His family. Now you as His child share in a heavenly inheritance! You are now one in Christ and joint heirs with Him according to the promises of Abraham found in chapter 28 of Deuteronomy. As you begin to read His Word and grow in the Lord, He will continue to work in changing your heart. You will daily be conformed to the image of Christ Himself. You will begin to live righteously and desire the will of the Father. Obedience to God will not be a burden to you, it will become a joy.

You may wonder, now that you have been born again, "What now?" My recommendations are these: **1.** Find a church that preaches the uncompromising Word and rejoice in the fellowship of other believers; 2. Study the Bible, for that is where we learn of God and His desires for you; **3.** Pray to Him to strengthen your faith and increase your love toward Him; and **4.** Enjoy the blessings of God that will begin coming your way. Be baptized as soon as possible as a testimony to God that you are symbolically dead to sin (the old life) and raised up clean for His service. May God richly bless you in your new walk with the Him.

CHAPTER 10

Is It God's Will for Us to Get Sick?

O nce we understand where sickness comes from, we can understand why we are able to get rid of it! God's word clearly reveals that both death and sickness originated with sin and are being spread by Satan. **Romans 5:12-21** *When Adam sinned, sin entered the entire human race. Adam's sin brought death; so death spread to everyone, for everyone sinned.* Yes, people sinned even before the law was given. And though there was no law to break, since it had not yet been given, they all died anyway—even though they did not disobey an explicit commandment of God, as Adam did. What a contrast between Adam and Christ, who was yet to come!

And what a difference between our sin and God's generous gift of forgiveness. For this one man, Adam, brought death to many through his sin. But this other man, Jesus Christ, brought forgiveness to many through God's bountiful gift. And the result of God's gracious gift is very different from the result of that one man's sin. For Adam's sin led to condemnation; but we have the free gift of being accepted by God, even though we are guilty of many sins.

The sin of this one man, Adam, caused death to rule over us, but all who receive God's wonderful, gracious gift of righteousness will live in triumph over sin and death through this one man, Jesus Christ.

Yes, Adam's one sin brought condemnation upon everyone, but Christ's one act of righteousness makes all people right in God's sight and gives them life. Because one person disobeyed God, many people became sinners. But because one other Person obeyed God, many people will be made right in God's sight.

God's law was given so that all people could see how sinful they are. But as people sinned more and more, God's wonderful kindness became more abundant. So just as sin ruled over all people and brought them to death, now God's wonderful kindness rules instead, giving us right standing with God and resulting in eternal life through Jesus Christ our Lord. **Luke 13:16** *And ought not this woman, being a daughter of Abraham, whom Satan has bound, lo, these eighteen years, be loosed from this bond on the Sabbath day?* Think of all those Jesus healed—they were all "oppressed of the devil." **Acts 10:38** *How God anointed Jesus of Nazareth with the Holy Ghost and with power: who went about doing good, and healing all that were oppressed of the devil; for God was with Him.*

John 5:14 *Behold, thou art made whole, sin no more, lest a worse thing come unto you.* **John 4:14** *But whosoever drinks of the water that I shall give him shall never thirst; but the water that I shall give him shall be in him, a well of water springing up into everlasting life.* Only when sin is taken out of the human race will there be no more sickness. **Revelation 21:3-5** *And I heard a great voice out of heaven saying, Behold, the tabernacle of God is with men, and he will dwell with them, and they shall be his people, and God himself shall be with them, and be their God. And God shall wipe away all tears from their eyes; and there shall be no* *more death, neither sorrow, nor crying, neither shall there be any more pain: for the former things are passed away. And He that sat upon the throne said, Behold I make all things new.* God's word teaches that forgiveness of sin and healing of the body go hand in hand. Healing is just as easy to receive from God as forgiveness of sin. If you have need of healing, it is only right that you surrender your life to God if you expect Him to heal you. The body is God's house as well as our own.

I Corinthians 6:19-20 *What? Know you not that your body is the temple of the Holy Ghost which is in you, which you have of God, and you are not your own? For you are bought with a price: therefore glorify God in your body, and in your spirit, which are God's.* Because it is God's house, we are forbidden to mar it, to defile it or to abuse it. **I Corinthians 3:15-17** *If any man's work shall be burned, he shall suffer loss; but he himself shall be saved; yet so as by fire. Know you not that you are the temple of God, and that the Spirit of God dwells in you? If any man defile the temple of God, him shall God destroy; for the temple of God is holy, which temple you are.*

SATAN'S OBJECTIVE

Satan's primary objective is to discredit God. Spoiling our bodies is one way he operates. Created in the image of God, we are caught in the middle of this spiritual battleground. Satan *as a roaring lion walks about seeking whom he may devour.* **I Peter 5:8** *Be sober, be vigilant; because your adversary the devil, as a roaring lion, walks about, seeking whom he may devour: whom resist steadfast in the faith, knowing that the same afflictions are accomplished in your brethren that are in the world.* He will devour you with disease and sickness if you let him. Our great advantage is that God sent His Son to destroy the works of the devil. **I John 3:8** *He that commits sin is of the devil: for the devil* *sinned from the beginning. For this purpose the Son of God was manifested, that He might destroy the works of the devil.* God through Jesus Christ will destroy Satan's evil works in your body!

Our failures come because of an imperfect understanding of God's word. God's word declares that, *you shall know the truth and the truth shall make you free,* **John 8:32.** Satan, your adversary, knows the truth better than you do. Until you discover and start claiming what is legally yours, Satan will continue his harassment and assault on your life. He knows your weak areas.

The Bible clearly reveals that God wants to be the *healer* of His people and declares His will to heal all those who obey Him. Christ's works of healing were not only to prove His divinity but were a part of His complete mission of fulfilling the will of God. *Lo, I come to do Your will, O God.* **Hebrews 10:9** *Then said he, lo, I come to do your will, O God. He takes away the first that he may establish the second* [sacrifice or covenant]. **Matthew 12:15** *Great multitudes followed Him, and He healed them all.* Jesus Himself is a revelation of the will of God. He did the will of God; He healed all who came to Him. He has an unchanging priesthood. **Hebrews 13:8** *Jesus Christ the same yesterday, and today, and forever.*

In **Matthew 8:16-17,** God's word tells us that Jesus *healed all that were sick; that it might be fulfilled, which was spoken by Isaiah the prophet, saying Himself took our infirmities, and bore our sicknesses.* If He bore them, then they rightfully and legally belong to Him and for us to take them upon our body is to be taking something that does not belong to us. In the material realm if one takes something that does not belong to him, he is classified as a thief. The same thing applies in the spiritual realm. If Christ took our sins, then sins do not belong to the believer; and as long as the believer has sins, Christ's atonement means nothing to him. If Christ took our sickness and pain, then they do not belong to the believer, and for a believer to have them is illegal and Christ's death in bearing them means nothing.

Matthew 1:21 *And she shall bring forth a son, and you shall call his name Jesus: for he shall save his people from their sins.* **2Corinthians 5:17-21** *Therefore if man be in Christ, he is a new creature: old things are passed away; behold all things are become new. And all things are of God, who has reconciled us to himself by Jesus Christ, and has given to us the ministry of reconciliation; to wit, that God was in Christ, reconciling the world unto himself, not imputing their trespasses unto them; and has committed unto us the word of reconciliation.* **IJohn 1:7-9** *But if we walk in the light, as He is in the light, we have fellowship with one another, and the blood of Jesus Christ His Son cleanses us from all sin. If we say that we have no sin, we deceive ourselves, and the truth is not in us. If we confess our sins, He is faithful and just to forgive us our sins, and to cleanse us from all unrighteousness.*

At the hands of unbelievers, Jesus, our **Lamb**, was beaten. On His body deep furrows were plowed by the awful Roman lash as it literally tore pieces of flesh from his back. **These were the stripes** by which, Isaiah and Peter say, **we were healed**. And they were laid on His **body**. This was the bearing of our sicknesses, and so, the provision was made for the healing of our body. Then they nailed Him to the cross and pierced His side. His blood ran down on the ground, *shed for many for the remission of sins,* **Matthew 26:28**. Jesus our Lamb suffered in two ways. He shed His blood on the cross for our salvation from sin, and He bore the stripes on His **body** for our healing from sickness. If you have let Him take your sins, won't you let Him take your sickness? Healing is part of your salvation; do not be cheated out of it any more than you would permit yourself to be cheated out of forgiveness of sins.

In **Deuteronomy 28**, we find sickness given as a part of the "curse." But **Galatians 3:13** declares that *Christ has redeemed us from the curse of the law*. Look for a moment to the sicknesses specifically stated in **Deuteronomy 28**: *pestilence, consumption, fever inflammation, extreme burning, hemorrhoids, the scab, the itch, madness, blindness, astonishment of heart, smite you in the knees, in the legs, sore botch, all the diseases of Egypt*. And as if these were not enough, verse 61 adds *every sickness and every plague which is not written in the book of this law*. Is there anything left uncovered? If you are carrying a disease, you are carrying a part of the curse. This should not be.

Deuteronomy 7:15 tells us that diseases belong to those that hate God: *And the Lord will take away from you all sickness and will put none of the evil diseases of Egypt, which you know, upon you; but will lay them upon all them that hate you*. If you truly feel that it is God's will for you to be sick, you have no business going to a doctor trying to get rid of the will of God! The will of God is expressed in the Lord's Prayer: *Your will be done*. God has set us free from the curse of the law through Christ Jesus our Lord for "whosoever will" meet the conditions and believe the Word. We may except ourselves, saying, "It is not His will," but God excepts no one. He is no respecter of persons. His promises are to all.

James 5:14 asks, *Is any* [not some] *sick among you?* God is as willing to heal as He is to forgive sins. The only hindrance in getting the full benefits of Calvary is unbelief and lack of appropriation of the blessing which Christ died to give to all men. **Isaiah 53:4-5** states, *surely he has borne our griefs, and carried our sorrows; yet we did esteem him stricken, smitten of God, and afflicted. But he was wounded for our transgressions; he was bruised for our iniquities: the chastisement of our peace was upon him; and with his stripes we are healed*. And then in **Matthew 8:16-17**: *When* *the evening was come, they brought unto Him many that were possessed with devils; and He cast out the spirits with His word, and healed all that were sick: that it might be fulfilled which was spoken by Isaiah the prophet, saying, Himself took our infirmities, and bore our sicknesses.* **IPeter 2:24** *Who his own self bore our sins in his own body on the tree, that we, being dead to sins, should live unto righteousness: by whose stripes you were healed.*

James 5:14-16 *Is any sick among you? Let him call for the elders of the church; and let them pray over him, anointing him with oil in the name of the Lord. And the prayer of faith shall save the sick, and the Lord shall raise him up; and if he has committed sins, they shall be forgiven him.* And finally, **3John 2** *Confess your faults one to another, and pray one for another, that you may be healed. The effectual fervent prayer of a righteous man avails much.*

The faith that we receive from God is based upon the knowledge of His will. You cannot receive healing by faith if there is any question whether or not healing is for you. With proper knowledge of the will of God, you should not pray: "Lord, heal me, if it be Your will." "If" implies doubt, and doubt cancels faith. Never be guilty of praying a useless, unbelieving prayer. Don't question whether it is God's will for you to be healed. The Lord's Prayer states that God's will be done on earth as it is in heaven. Is heaven filled with sick people? Healing and health is God's will!

Our will, also, has a part in the question of healing. Will we take that which God has willed to give us? *If you abide in Me, and My words abide in you, you shall ask what you desire, and it shall be done for you.* **John 15:7** When our "I will" meets His "I will," the work is done.

HOW TO BE HEALED

You have the right and authority to claim healing from God when **1. you are a born-again Christian: Matthew**

13:15 states, *For this people's heart is waxed gross, and their ears are dull of hearing, and their eyes they have closed; lest at any time they should see with their eyes, and hear with their ears, and should understand with their heart, and should be converted, and I should heal them. . .* 2. **you are diligently listening to God: Exodus 15:26** *And He said, "If you will diligently hearken to the voice of the Lord your God, and will do that which is right in his sight, and will give ear to his commandments, and keep all his statutes, I will put none of these diseases upon you, which I have brought upon the Egyptians; for I am the Lord that heals you.". . .* **3. you are attending to God's word: Proverbs 4:20-22** *My son, attend to my words; incline your ear unto my sayings. Let them not depart from your eyes; keep them in the midst of your heart. For they are life unto those that find them, and health to all their flesh. . . .*and **4. your faith is unwavering**. But let him ask in faith, nothing wavering: **James 1:6-7** *For he that wavers is like a wave of the sea driven with the wind and tossed. For let not that man think that he shall receive any thing of the Lord.*

Now don't give up if you don't have enough faith—you can get it! Not everyone believes perfectly every time. *Faith comes by hearing, and hearing by the word of God.* Fill yourself with the appropriate word of God! *Let the words of my mouth and the meditation of my heart be acceptable in Your sight, O Lord my strength, and my redeemer*—**Psalm 19:14.** Speak the following verses boldly, over and over, and you will become a changed person. Your life will become hidden in Christ. Don't read them quietly, but read them aloud! You are building your own faith! Break your silence with God's unchanging Word:

Never confess that I can't—Say:
- *I can do all things through Christ who strengthens me.* **Philippians 4:13**

- *The Lord is the strength of my life.* **Psalm 27:1**
- *Oh Lord, my strength, and my stronghold, and my refuge in the day of affliction.* **Jeremiah 16:19**

Never confess that you lack—Say:

- *My God shall supply all of my needs according to His riches in Glory by Christ Jesus.* **Philippians 4:19**
- *No good thing will He withhold from them that walk uprightly.* **Psalm 84:11**

Never confess that you fear—Say:

- *For God has not given me the spirit of fear: but of power, and of love, and of a sound mind.* **2 Timothy 1:7**
- *Fear thou not! For I am with you: be not dismayed for I am your God. I will strengthen you: yea, I will help you: yea, I will uphold you with the right hand of my righteousness.* **Isaiah 41:10**

Never confess that you lack faith—Say:

- *God has dealt to every man the measure of faith.* **Romans 12:3**
- *For it is God which works in you both to will and to do for His good pleasure.* **Philippians 2:13**
- *For we are His workmanship, created in Christ.* **Ephesians 2:10**

Never confess your weakness or the supremacy of the devil—Say:

- *When the enemy shall come in like a flood, the Spirit of the Lord shall lift up a standard against him.* **Isaiah 59:19**
- *Behold I give you power over all the power of the enemy: and nothing shall by any means hurt you.* **Luke 10:19**

Never again confess defeat—Say:
- *Greater is He that is in me, than He that is in the world.* **I.John 4:4**
- *Thanks be unto God, which always causes us to triumph in Christ.* **2Corinthians 2:14**
- *In all things we are more than conquerors through Him that loved us.* **Romans 8:37**

Never again confess your sickness—Say:
- *Jesus. . .by whose stripes you were HEALED!*
- *I am the Lord that heals you.* **Exodus 15:26**
- *Bless the Lord, O My Soul. . . .who heals all your diseases.* **Psalm 103:1-3**
- *In my name, they shall lay hands on the sick, and they SHALL RECOVER.* **Mark 16:18**

NOW CLAIM WHAT IS YOURS!

When believers agree together, things begin to happen. Join with others in agreeing upon your condition, pray one for another, and get anointed with oil. **Mark 6:13** *And they cast out many devils, and anointed with oil many that were sick, and healed them.* **James 5:14-16** *Is any sick among you? Let him call for the elders of the church; and let them pray over him, anointing him with oil in the name of the Lord: And the prayer of faith shall save the sick, and the Lord shall raise him up; and if they have committed sins, they shall be forgiven him. Confess your faults one to another, and pray one for another, that you may be healed. The effectual fervent prayer of a righteous man avails much.*

Jesus referred to healing as "Children's Bread." If sinners can get the crumbs (and many are being saved and healed at the same time), you are entitled to your share. **Matthew 15:26** *But he answered and said, It is not meet to take the children's bread, and to cast it to dogs.* **James 4:7** *Resist the devil and he will flee from you.* Tell Satan **aloud** that he is overcome by the blood of the Lamb, and by the word of your testimony! **Revelation 12:11** *And they overcame him by the blood of the Lamb, and by the word of their testimony; and they loved not their lives unto the death.* Then tell him that you are washed clean by the blood of Jesus and that by His stripes **you are healed**, that you refuse to accept Satan's baggage which belongs to those who hate God.

As you win the battle and symptoms disappear, prepare for the counter-attack! Satan does not give up easily. He will attack with a pain or an old symptom in the healed area to try and strike fear and doubt in your heart. This is a test of your faith. It is vital that you do not deny your healing and accept the condition again. Immediately strike back with the Word of God. When you resist him he must flee! Repeat the faith-building verses. The more you say them, the more you believe. The less you say them, the less you believe.

There is no power that Jesus exercised in His ministry which every true believer cannot have today. True believers can heal the sick and cast out devils! They can perform miracles and raise the dead. Many will say these things were only for the Apostles, just to get the church started. No, my friend, this is what **you** were meant to be and do! Jesus said in **John 14:12** *HE THAT BELIEVES ON ME THE WORKS THAT I DO SHALL HE DO ALSO; AND GREATER WORKS THAN THESE SHALL HE DO.* When we believe this, we see miracles!

CHAPTER 11

A Challenge to Believers

My hope is that if you do not currently have a burden for the lost, you soon **will** have through the information and revelation found in this chapter. Be absolutely sure you are soundly saved. The Apostle Paul said to *work out your own salvation with fear and trembling* (**Philippians 2:12**). How much fear and trembling do you experience in your Christian walk? Is it all sweetness and love? You may say, but God is "all LOVE" — NO! He is a righteous God and cannot tolerate sin. In fact, the Word says that the sinner is an enemy of God. This chapter is to help you get a proper perspective of who God is... the other side of the coin!

The Fear of the Lord

Philippians 2:12 *Wherefore, my beloved, as you have always obeyed, not as in my presence only, but now much more in my absence, work out your own salvation with fear and trembling.*

Psalms 2:11 *Serve the LORD with fear, and rejoice with trembling.* **1 Corinthians 2:3-5** *And I was with you in weakness, and in fear, and in much trembling. And my speech and my preaching was not with enticing words of man's wisdom, but in demonstration of the Spirit and of power: that your* *faith should not stand in the wisdom of men, but in the power of God.*

Psalms 111:9-10 *He sent redemption unto his people: he has commanded his covenant forever; holy and revered is his name. 111:10 The fear of the LORD is the beginning of wisdom: a good understanding have all they that do his commandments; his praise endures forever.*

Psalms 112:1 *Praise you the LORD. Blessed is the man that fears the LORD, that delights greatly in his commandments.* **Psalms 112:7** *He shall not be afraid of evil tidings; his heart is fixed, trusting in the LORD.* **Matthew 10:28** *And fear not them which kill the body, but are not able to kill the soul; but rather fear him [God] which is able to destroy both soul and body in hell.*

Prophecy speaks to the intellect of the sinner, while the law speaks to the conscience. One produces faith in the word of God; the other brings knowledge of sin in the heart of the sinner. The law is the God-given "key" to unlock the treasure of salvation. The law of the Lord is perfect converting the soul... it is the **law of the Lord** that actually converts the soul, not love.

Matthew 7:13-23 *Enter you in at the straight gate; for wide is the gate, and broad is the way, that leads to destruction, and many are there that go in. Because straight is the gate, and narrow is the way, which leads unto life, and few there be that find it. Beware of false prophets, which come to you in sheep's clothing, but inwardly they are ravening wolves. You shall know them by their fruits. Do men gather grapes of thorns, or figs or thistles? Even so every good tree brings forth good fruit; but a corrupt tree brings forth evil fruit. A good tree cannot bring forth evil fruit; neither can a corrupt tree bring forth good fruit. Every tree that that does not bring forth good fruit is hewn down, and cast into the fire. Wherefore by their fruits you shall know them. Not everyone that says unto Me, "Lord, Lord," shall enter into* *the kingdom of heaven; but he that does the will of My Father which is in heaven.*

You say you know the Lord? That's not good enough... the devil and his demons know Him better than you do and they will be spending an eternity in hell!

Matthew 7:22 Many *will say to me in that day, Lord, Lord, have we not prophesied in your name? And in your name have cast out devils? And in your name done many wonderful works? And then will I profess unto them, I never knew you: depart from me, you that work iniquity.*

Revelation 3:15-16 *I know your works, that you are neither cold nor hot: I would prefer that you be cold or hot. So, because you are lukewarm, and neither cold nor hot, I will vomit you out of my mouth.* **Matthew 5:29-30** *And if your right eye offend you, pluck it out, and cast it from thee; for it is profitable for you that one of your members should perish, and not that your whole body should be cast into hell. And if your right hand offend you, cut it off, and cast it from you; for it is profitable for you that one of your members should perish, and not that your whole body should be cast into hell.* **Luke 12:5** *But I will forewarn you whom you shall fear: Fear Him, which after He has killed has power to cast into hell; yea, I say unto you, FEAR HIM!*

To not fear God is not only unscriptural, it is irreverent. **Matthew 25:41** *Then shall he say also unto them on the left hand, Depart from me, you cursed, into everlasting fire, prepared for the devil and his angels.* **John 14:15** *If you love me, you will keep my commandment,* says Jesus to us today. We could say that is a very strong statement by Jesus. Does this mean that every time we sin we do not love Jesus? Yes. Although we love Jesus, every time we commit sin we love something or someone else more than Jesus. If we love Jesus more than anything else, we will keep ourselves free from sin for Jesus. If we love Jesus we will strive to give ourselves totally to Him.

When we sin we are giving ourselves to something or somebody other than Jesus. God is jealous. **Exodus 34:14** For *you shall worship no other god: for the LORD, whose name is Jealous, is a jealous God.* **Deuteronomy 4:24** For *the LORD your God is a consuming fire, even a jealous God.* **Deuteronomy 5:9** *You shall not bow down thyself unto them, nor serve them; for I the LORD your God am a jealous God, visiting the iniquity of the fathers upon the children unto the third and fourth generation of them that hate me.* **Nahum 1:2** *God is jealous, and the LORD revenges; the LORD revenges, and is furious; the LORD will take vengeance on his adversaries, and He reserves wrath for His enemies.* **James 4:4** *You adulterers and adulteresses, know you not that the friendship of the world is enmity with God? Whosoever therefore will be a friend of the world is the enemy of God.*

When we love Jesus with all our heart, soul, mind and strength we will not want to put anything, no matter how small, before Jesus. I repeat the words of Jesus in our Gospel, "If you love Me you will keep my commandments." Sometimes we hear people make statements like, "Jesus understands that I am human. He will forgive me." Jesus is forgiving; we do not doubt Jesus' mercy. But if we love Jesus more than anything, we will put Jesus before whatever it is that is tempting us and try to root that sin out of our lives completely.

God would not have said, *be you Holy for I am Holy*, if it were not possible! (**Leviticus 11: 44-45; 19:2; 20:7; 20:26**) Loving Jesus, therefore, is not just something emotional; loving Jesus means changing our lives, reforming our lives, working on our personalities and characters, overcoming sinful habits, stretching ourselves to love as Jesus loved. Loving Jesus means thinking about ourselves and others as Jesus thinks.

Where does your information about yourself and others and the world come from? If it comes only from "Hellavision" or

"Hellywood" and a materialistic western culture which does not understand the difference between freedom to sin and the freedom to do what is right, our minds may be contaminated by false images of ourselves, others and the world. But if we truly want to love Jesus, we will fill our minds with His thoughts and His way of looking at the world.

We can fill our minds with Jesus' thoughts by reading the Bible, reading spiritual books and praying as much as possible every day. **1Corinthians 2:16** *For who has known the mind of the Lord, that he may instruct him? But we have the mind of Christ.*

If we fill our minds with the filth of the world, how can we love Jesus? It would be impossible, and it would be impossible to keep his commandments. Let us fill our minds with the thoughts of Jesus so that we may love Him and keep His commandments as He commanded us to do. Remember one of the most important commandments, **Mark 16:15** *And he said unto them, Go you into all the world, and preach the gospel to every creature.* If you truly believe that God is, then you will believe what He says: that there is a day of wrath and eternal punishment for those who are not born again. And if you believe that, you should be trying to warn others!

"Have you no wish for others to be saved? Then you are not saved yourself, be sure of that." Charles Spurgeon

Pray that God will give you a revelation of who He is and a burden for the lost! Start first with your family. Amen

A Personal Testimony

My name is Douglas Hoover. Am I famous, well known, a celebrity, popular preacher, evangelist or pastor of a renowned megachurch? No. Then why should you listen to anything I have to say or spend time reading about my opinion of what the Book of Job is about? This is a fair question.

I believed Jesus when He said that all have sinned by breaking God's Laws, and that the penalty for sin is death and Hell, the place prepared for Satan and the rest of the fallen angels. Now if I said I believed this to be true, wouldn't my life and communication reflect that fact by my warning others of this pending doom? Of course it would, and it does. Rarely does a day go by that I neglect handing someone a tract or saying something to them; and I regularly encourage my brothers and sisters in Christ to do the same.

I believed Jesus when He said that He took my sins on the cross along with my sickness, disease and infirmities, and that if place my trust and faith in Him, salvation, healing and health would be mine as a free gift from God. Now if I said I believed this to be true, wouldn't my life and communication reflect that fact? Wouldn't I be claiming and proclaiming my salvation, health and healing? If that is what I am professing and I'm walking around sick and defeated, wouldn't you question my claims of faith in this doctrine? A question such as: Hey, if Jesus took your sickness, on the cross to free you from the curse of sickness, then why are you sick? This is a fair question. I would answer, either Jesus is a liar or I don't truly believe what He said.

I believed Jesus when He said, by my stripes you were healed, …I sent my word and healed them …God's Will be done on earth, as it is in heaven, …these signs will follow all those who believe… they will lay hands on the sick and they will recover, …ask anything in My name believing and I will give it to you that the Father in Heaven will be Glorified through the Son Jesus Christ. Guess what? I believe, and these signs follow me! By the blood of Jesus Christ and by the resurrection power in that blood, sickness has to flee when I command it to. My body is the temple of God and the dwelling place for the Holy Spirit; sickness, disease, infirmities, fear, anxiety have no place and have to flee.

I believed Jesus when He said, if I seek first the Kingdom of God and His Righteousness, then all these things will be added unto me. What things? you might ask. The Father knows what you have need of and He also will give you the (Godly) desires of your heart… no plague will come near your dwelling… whatever you put your hands to will prosper… you shall have and not want… your cupboards will be full… flocks will be many… angels will be encamped around about you to protect you from harm… your enemies will scatter… you will have a long life free of sickness… So, what do you have need of? Simply start seeking God and His Righteousness and you will have it.

Do you have sickness, disease, calamity, infirmity, poverty or lack, about to lose your home, spouse, family member, loved one, job, or other source of security; are you blaming God? If you are, and you haven't read this book, read it! If you are still blaming God after reading this book, you need to read it again. Job blamed God, and where did it get him? It is not God's fault; it is your MOUTH and POISONOUS TONGUE! Put some super glue on your lips and start reading this book again!

I have not been sick since I discovered these truths!

In the winter of 1981, I was installing a shingle roof on a two-story house on the Washash Front, east of Salt Lake City. On this cold, rainy morning, we were preparing to install the rolls of felt paper on the roof sheeting and upon donning my yellow plastic pants and rain jacket. I started climbing the 36-foot extension latter. The siding had yet to be applied so there were only bracing sheets at the corners leaving the balance of the house interior exposed. As I passed the second floor a plumber working in an upstairs bathroom caught my attention by reminding me of the approaching storm heading our way from the west. He stated in constructing worker's vocabulary, that we "were [%?!*#] for going up on the roof today." The bible says in Hosea 6:4 *My people are destroyed for a lack of knowledge.* I was not aware of the power of my words and how I can open up the door for Satan to kill, steal and destroy. I should have cast down the next thought that crossed my mind, because it did not line up with the truth of God's word. I could have given God the glory by quoting the Bible, that God has given the angels charge over me, protecting me from harm. But no, I had to be cute and funny, get a laugh! I simply said four words. "Make it University Hospital."

Twenty minutes later we got hit by the storm; it wasn't rain but sleet and it stuck to the felt. I panicked and started to scoot down the roof and the plastic pants afored no traction; in seconds I was traveling so fast that my heels ripped out the 2x4 that was nailed along the eave for protection from just such an event. As I started sliding down the roof, I turned and grabbed onto a 50-pound box of roofing nails in hopes of it halting my descent. No such thing. I now had a 50-pound companion along for the ride, adding a 12-foot 2x4 just prior to rocketing off the roof at the 28-foot level.

Do I believe in angels? Yes I do! I landed on frozen rocky ground, on my back, and ended up in the University Hospital twenty minutes after telling the plumber where I was expecting to be. What was the extent of my injuries? Only two cracked vertebrae. I discovered there were two others who fell besides me, one who broke his back and is a paraplegic, and one whot died. Do I believe in angels? Yes I do! Do I believe in the power of words? Yes I do! (You may ask, did Satan push me off the roof? No. Did I open up the door for the spirit of fear with my comment, "Make it University Hospital"? Yes I did. Did he plant the spirit of fear with the thought, "You had better get off the roof right away"? Yes. God's wisdom or the mind of Christ would say, "Sit still until the storm blows over, the sleet will melt in minutes." Which it did! I listened to Satan's voice through the door of fear and anxiety.)

We are subject to God's Spiritual Laws just as much as we are the laws of nature. You have a free will to defy nature's laws or God's Laws. If you choose to, don't blame God for the outcome as Job did.

There can be serious consequences for not operating in faith. You must know: Hebrews 11:6 But *without faith it is impossible to please God: for he that comes to God must believe that he is, and that he rewards those that diligently seek him.* It is not a matter of whether God is allowing something to happen to you; He has no choice, He must honor His Laws. If you are ignorant of His laws, it does not make them of non-effect, there are still consequences. That is why He said, *My people are destroyed for a lack of knowledge.* God is not destroying; He is not even permitting or allowing it! YOU ARE, by the words of your mouth, speaking fear and unbelief, so again, DON"T BLAME GOD OR EVEN GIVE HIM CREDIT!

Do you want healing? Stop confessing sickness! Do you want prosperity? Stop speaking and confessing and

proclaiming lack! You are giving the glory, credit and attention to Satan who has *come but to kill, steal and destroy.*
Do you think that pleases God? *Without words of faith,
it is impossible to please Him*! Do you want victory? Try
professing, "Greater is He that is in me than he that is in the
world." "I can do all things through Christ who strengthens
me." You just read these two scriptures, but understand this,
Faith comes by hearing and hearing by the word of God.
You need to "hear" the Word of God not just read it. Every
cell of your body needs to hear you say it. Your spirit is in
charge of your body; your body does not control your spirit.
Your brain takes what your ears hear and sends commands
to every cell of your body. Start sending the right commands
to your ears: God's Word, the Truth of the Word, the Power
of the Word, the Life in the Word, Healing and Health in the
Word, Victory in the Word! So say these scriptures again, out
loud! Don't even think about what someone in the room or
earshot might say, what matters is what God says.

Now say this OUT LOUD: "Greater is He that is in me
than he that is in the world." "I can do all things through
Christ who strengthens me." "No weapon formed against me
shall prosper." "God forgive me for not putting You first in
my life and serving other gods, and I have opened up the door
for Satan to kill, steal and destroy. Wash me clean from my
guilt. Purify me from my sin. For I recognize my shameful
deeds- they haunt me day and night. Against You, and You
alone, have I sinned; I have done what is evil in Your sight.
You will be proved right in what you say, and your judgment
against me is just. For I was born a sinner—yes, from the
moment my mother conceived me. But you desire honesty
from the heart, so you can teach me to be wise in my inmost
being. Purify me from my sins, and I will be clean; wash me,
and I will be whiter than snow. Oh, give me back my joy
again; you have broken me—now let me rejoice. Don't keep
looking at my sins. Remove the stain of my guilt. Create in

me a clean heart, O God. Renew a right spirit within me. Do not banish me from your presence, and don't take your Holy Spirit from me. Restore to me again the joy of your salvation, and make me willing to obey you. Then I will teach your ways to sinners, and they will return to you. Unseal my lips, O Lord, that I may praise you. I want to start giving You the first part of every day with prayer and bible study for You have said that if I seek first Your kingdom and Your righteousness, You will provide all of my needs. Lord, I pray You will help my unbelief. I promise to hide Your word in my heart, that I will not sin against you. Thank you, Lord Jesus, for hearing my prayer."

Okay, you can read to yourself now.

In 2001 I was working on a live electrical circuit and prior to commencement of work the Holy Spirit clearly told me to de-energize the circuit first before working on it. I argued that I have worked on hundreds of live circuits in the past and knew what I was doing. I did not listen and commenced removing the junction box cover. I failed to notice a copper water pipe running alongside the junction box and a copper water line is a perfect electrical ground. As I started to strip the insulation off the hot wire, my finger slipped off the insulated handle of the stripper that had just cut through the wire insulation, my bare right arm was resting on the copper waterline.

I suddenly realized I was paralyzed by electrocution and could not move or let go of the stripper and there was no doubt in my mind I was going to die because I was thinking about how glad I was that I had taken out a very substantial life insurance policy and other morbid topics. Instantly I became aware that it was my upper body that was paralyzed and that the current was flowing from my left arm to my right arm to ground. I managed to lift my leg up and put it against the wall and pushed. I fell and landed on my shoulder blades, ripping the rotator cuff muscles from the shoulder bones. The MRI results confirmed the doctor's suspicions and surgery was recommended for the purpose of reattaching the muscles to the humerus bone. I explained to the doctor that I believed God for healing and declined the surgery, so they recommended trying physical therapy to try and ease the pain. But after three months there was no change.

Again they tried to talk me into surgery and I said God was my healer. Over the next four months, I had to sleep on my back and since I could not lift my arms, Alice had to help me get dressed. In the spring of 2002, I was on the 34th day of a 40-day fast and while praying for healing for a lady with cancer, God instantly healed me as I knelt by my bed. He instantly reattached the rotator cuff muscles to the bones! The doctors at the VA Medical Center all agreed that it is impossible for a tendon to reattach itself to bone, let alone two at once! They explained that the only way was to drill holes in the bone and suture the tendon to it through the holes.

PRAISE GOD, HIS WORD IS TRUTH! Not only did God heal me, He instantaneously healed the lady of her cancer! She was scheduled for surgery the following day and during post-op realized her tongue was no longer cancerous; a biopsy was called for immediately and no cancer cells were discovered! GOD IS GREAT!

In the fall of 2006 I was seriously injured in a fall. We had constructed a concrete cool-off pool 6 feet deep and 12 feet wide; in the center was an 8-inch diameter concrete pillar protruding from the floor to the surface. On top of the pillar was a 3-foot wide flat piece of quartzite rock which served as a turtle island. Because this flat rock was on the surface of the water, it was not possible to see that it was no longer cemented on center to the concrete pillar. Not only was the quartzite not attached to the pillar, it was sitting off center a whole 12 inches. I was planning to take a short-cut by jumping out to the quartzite island and then across to the other side. As I backed up to take a run at it, the Holy Spirit told me not to do it, to walk around the outside. I ignored Him and continued to position myself for the assault. As I started to run, the voice came again louder, much like during the electrocution incident. I instantly reasoned and argued that I knew what I was doing, and would simply land with my foot in the center so as to be directly over the top of the pillar. As my foot landed with 250 pounds of force on the quartzite, I instantly realized as the rock gave way and flipped down that it was off-center a foot towards me.

As both feet plunged into the water, the momentum of my running carried me forward and my chest came down directly over the concrete pillar which quickly impacted my rib cage. My breath was instantly forced from my lungs and I felt an excruciating pain in my chest, realizing I indeed cracked and broke some ribs. It was all I could do to climb the face of the water fall to get out of the pool. I am screaming out in pain as I was trying to suck air into my lungs. My home-owners were not home nor were the neighbors on either side of them. If they had been, they would have thought I had lost my mind. I was walking in circles, holding my chest, bent over with horrid pain, gasping for air, soaked from head to foot and screaming a prayer to Jesus. "Thank you Jesus for your healing, I love you Lord, help me Jesus, I praise you for your goodness and mercy, help me Jesus, thank you for my healing," gasping, crying, coughing, pleading, begging and praising the whole time. Like I said, I anyone heard me they would have thought I was crazy!

I headed for my truck in the front of the house and by the time I reached it I thought I was going to pass out from the pain and lack of oxygen. As I pulled out of the cul-de-sac and stopped at the end of the street to pull out onto the main road, I realized that Palomar Hospital was less than a mile down the road to the right. My brain was flooded with a thousand thoughts, some good, some bad, some crazy, some sad, some terrifying, such as "What are you doing, what are you saying, are you insane, believe God? You need to get to the hospital, you're going to pass out on the highway if you try to drive home. If you even make it home, does your wife have faith to believe God can heal you, do you have faith? If you did He would have already done it. Turn right you idiot! Get to the hospital! You can't breathe, you can't think straight. Praise God I'm healed! No you aren't! I love you God! He doesn't love you! You're an idiot! It's all your fault! I can't breathe, I'm going to pass out."

By God's grace and mercy I made it home; I walked into the house soaking wet and ashen-faced, holding my chest, crying and trying to desperately put one foot in front of the other and breathe. "I hurt myself," was all I could manage to breathe out. Alice helped me get my wet clothes off and, with great difficulty, sit down on the bed. It was too painful to try and lie down so I sat, propped up with pillows. As I became rested it was a little painful to breathe. My chest had an 8- inch red circle from the impact with the concrete pillar and the entire area was already black and purple. Alice spent most of the night praying for me and when I was coherent, we both would pray. At about 5 oclock in the morning, Alice helped me to the bathroom and we discovered blood in my urine.

Satan had a ball with that discovery. I got back to the bed and realized that I had only been kidding myself about feeling better, for the truth was I could hardly bear to breathe, and now this. Satan assured me that even though it had been over 18 months since God healed your shoulders, it was merely psychosomatic and that is why you were feeling pain in your shoulders when you woke up this morning. So here you lay with broken and fractured ribs, internal injuries, and torn rotator cuff muscles that were never healed in the first place. You probably have a punctured lung and you're bleeding to death. At that moment I screamed out Satan,

"You're a liar and I trust my Lord and my healer!" Alice was startled and just continued to pray. Immediately after saying this, the Holy Spirit plainly said that I needed to repent and ask forgiveness, and that I was in this state because I did not obey the warning of the Holy Spirit. I instantly cried out, "Lord, forgive me for not listening or obeying you, I am to blame for my condition and I can't blame anyone but myself!" The second I repented, God instantly restored me to perfect health. The red circle from the impact and all the bruises and pain were gone and I could thump on my chest with my fists like Tarzan! As I threw my arms up to heaven and began praising God, I suddenly realized the symptons in my shoulders were also gone. Alice said I walked around the house for 45 minutes praising God with my hands in the air, and to me it seemed like 5 minutes. You can't have miracles like these happen to you without it changing your life!

August 4, 2007 was the next major change in our walk with God. I had finally reached the point in my life where everything that appeared to be important seemed more like vanity. A terrorizing thought plagued my mind: How many people would show up at my funeral, and what would they have to say about me? "Boy, Doug Hoover sure did build a lot of beautiful waterfalls and could always seem to find a way to make you laugh." That's it? Was anyone's life improved in any way because Doug Hoover was on the earth? Did he ease anybody's pain or heartache, did he help the poor or homeless, the down and out or comfort the sick and dying? Was anyone's life enriched because Doug Hoover lived? Was one person saved or introduced to Jesus by Doug Hoover? Did someone find hope or a renewed faith in God because Doug Hoover took time to think of someone other than himself?

Well, on Sunday morning, August 5th at 11:30, I made a commitment to God to dedicate the rest of my life to Him and to start every day by putting Him first in prayer and in the study of His Word. My wife and I decided to sell everything we owned, including our house, to buy a motor home and live for Jesus on the road, witnessing and ministering to everyone we meet. We asked God for a motor home and asked Him to pay off all our debts so we could be totally free to serve Him.

On August 12th, I met a man in order to give him a bid on a waterfall project. Alice went with me because it was after church that we were to meet. After talking business he and his wife went out to dinner with us and in our conversation we mentioned we were buying a motor home. They then suggested that we park it on their two acres while I built the project.

On Monday, August 13th, we got a call from the motor home dealership where we "in faith" made an offer on a $150,000 Winnebago "Ultimate Advantage." We needed to come up with $50,000 for a down payment and believed God would come through miraculously. They said our application was approved and we could come in with the deposit the next day.

The second call on the 13th was from the man I had just met on the 12th for the waterfall bid. He asked me if I would like to pay cash for my motor home. I was shocked at his question, especially when he added, "Can you come up with $5,000 in 24 hours?" I didn't ask him why, I just felt by the Spirit that God had a hand in this. So I simply said, "Yes," trusting that whatever he was up to was in God's will. He replied, "I'll call you right back." He didn't call me back until the 14th when he explained he had purchased several thousand shares of stock in a medical company at a dollar per share. Another acquaintance had called him on the 13th to ask if he would buy her shares at one dollar each (what she had paid for them the year before) because she needed the cash. He explained to me that he knew another company was interested in buying this one, so he was sure it would be a good deal, and that this stock had been purchased and owned prior to the acquisition, therefore a totally legal trade. So he called a few of his friends and told them of the offer and he said we came to mind. However, he went ahead and bought 5000 shares of stock for us with his own money and said he would take the risk for us. So when he called me on Tuesday he announced he had bought us 5000 shares for a dollar each so I owed him $5,000. Then he added, this company was bought out today at $55 a share, so you just received $285,000.00!

The third call on the 13th was from a proposal I delivered a week before on a $200,000 waterfall; they had decided to go ahead with the proposal and I could pick up the check for the down payment of $75,000 on the 14th. There was our $50,000 deposit for the motor home we were believing God for on the 14th! In 10 days from commiting our lives to God, we got our motor home, the $50,000 deposit, and paid it off the same day with the $200,000.00 waterfall project, which netted close to $150,000.00. Then He brought a stranger into our lives that paid off all our debts by having God touch his heart. Do you see now why I have written this book? How could I not?

Doug Hoover is not a celebrity, or anyone famous, but he is a child of God who has decided to take God at his Word and place his faith and trust in Him and to seek first His Kingdom and His Righteousness and "all these things are being added unto him"!

Presenting your body to God as a living sacrifice requires submitting your will and the emotions to the direction of the Holy Spirit. Your mind needs to be conformed to the **Word of God** so that it can cooperate with the leading of the Holy Spirit. God speaks to our spirit by his Holy Spirit which, in turn, directs the soul (mind, will, emotions); and the mind directs the body, which includes our mouth. Now you can be a true ambassador for God!

Pray that God will give you a revelation of who He is and a burden for the lost! Start first with your family. Amen

Please make a difference in this world with the time you have left,

My Love To You,
Doug Hoover

Printed in the United States
106329LV00002B/190-501/P